Dictionary of Obscenity
& Taboo

The Wordsworth
Dictionary of Obscenity
& Taboo

–

James McDonald

Wordsworth Reference

First published in Great Britain by Sphere Books Ltd, 1988.

This edition published 1996 by Wordsworth Editions Ltd.
Cumberland House, Crib Street, Ware, Hertfordshire SG12 9ET.

ISBN 1-85326-371-0

Printed and bound in Great Britain by Mackays of Chatham PLC.

INTRODUCTION

The principal purpose of words is to enable us to communicate with each other, but in performing this rôle they affect us in many ways. We might be delighted, amused, or intrigued by them. We might even be disgusted by them.

In many ways it is the words which disgust and offend that are the most interesting. How can it be that anyone can be offended by a simple, harmless word?

Take, for example, *fuck*, a word familiar to almost all adult native speakers of English. Is it the ugly sound of the word that makes it objectionable, as Mrs Mary Whitehouse has suggested? (letter to the *Independent*, 2 November 1987). Clearly not. If it were then we should expect people to be offended by hearing the word before they knew its meaning. In fact children, unworldly adults, and foreigners who are not yet familiar with it find it as euphonious as any other word. Furthermore, if the sound was really so important we might expect Mrs Whitehouse to avoid rhyming words such as *duck*, *luck*, and *puck*.

Is it, then, something to do with the particular combination of letters in the written word? Again, clearly not. Mrs Whitehouse would be equally offended by *fuc*, *fuk*, or *phuck*. Also, if the aesthetic appearance of the written word was the critical factor then we should expect the combination to be avoided in other languages. In fact it may be found in many non-English speaking countries, sometimes as an ordinary everyday word, sometimes in random letter combinations such as car registration marks (in Britain vehicle registration marks are carefully censored to eliminate such combinations).

If the source of the offence is not the sound or spelling of the word *fuck*, what is it? Is it perhaps the meaning? Certainly the meaning seems to have something to do with it, but this cannot be the whole story. If it were then we should expect expressions such as *copulate* and *make love* to be considered just as outrageous.

In some parts of the English-speaking world words like *prick*, *cunt*, and *fuck* are perfectly acceptable, but *penis*, *vagina*, and *sexual intercourse* are highly offensive.[1] The reason is, apparently, that when the words were introduced to such places they were accompanied by the attitudes of the people who introduced them. The former were taught by sailors and traders who treated sex as a perfectly natural fact of life, the latter by Christian missionaries who regarded sex as shameful.

The truth of it is that words become taboo by tacit common consent. If everyone accepts that a certain word should be regarded as beyond the pale, then it is; if we all agreed that the word *tea-pot* were obscene, then it would be. This process is well illustrated by the word *bloody*. As an exclamation *bloody* is a totally meaningless word with an uncertain etymology. Yet this harmless, vacuous word generated genuine outrage and disgust in 1912 when it was first used on the stage, in Shaw's *Pygmalion*. Even today it can cause deep offence in certain quarters, though the people who are so deeply offended can give no sustainable reason for their reaction.

In other cultures various different subjects are taboo. Popular ones around the world include men's mothers-in-law, women's fathers-in-law, royalty, left-handedness, certain dangerous animals, supernatural beings, and eating. Most societies share our taboos concerning incest, and many have taboos concerning altered states of consciousness. These typically cover sleep and dreams, drunkenness, drugged states, insanity, fever, and the most severe alteration to any state of consciousness: death.

We are at liberty to select our own taboos as long as we can muster a consensus. In practice, therefore, our chosen taboos reflect our communal attitudes, and the fact that in recent times English speakers have tended to stigmatize sex and excretion must say something about our collective mentality. The problem is that no one quite knows what. Whatever the reason, new English words associated with sex and excretion still tend to become taboo. As they do so fresh euphemisms are introduced to take their places. Soon the process affects these new terms and they are displaced in turn. The inevitable life cycle of these words is as follows: euphemism, popular English, colloquialism, vulgarism, obscenity.

Euphemism is the inevitable partner of taboo. It is not a peculiarly English phenomenon. Indeed, euphemism is used extensively through-

[1] John Money, *MIMS Magazine*, Vol. 3, No. 5, 15 September 1978, 'Dirt and Dirty in Sexual Talk and Behaviour.'

out the world, and has been throughout recorded history. The very word *euphemism* is of ancient Greek origin; it denoted, as it does now, an auspicious term used in place of an inauspicious one. One of the most striking euphemisms of all is a Greek one. The Furies, a group of terrifying primal Greek goddesses, were properly called the *Erinyes*, but they were so feared that their name was rarely used. Instead they were generally known as the *Eumenides*, 'the kindly ones'.

Our Germanic ancestors avoided words for particularly fearsome animals. Their word for a bear, for example, is unknown because it was never recorded, though from philological evidence we can be reasonably certain that such a word existed. *Bear* itself is a euphemism for this missing word: it means 'the brown one'. So too in Anglo–Saxon times, when death was an ever-present threat, the ancestor of the modern word *die* was taboo. It was written down for the first time only after the Norman Conquest.

By the fourteenth century some words explicitly associated with sex were starting to become taboo. Chaucer, for example, never used the word *cunt*, although he freely employed equally explicit synonyms.

Shakespeare, writing in the late sixteenth and early seventeenth centuries, avoided the words *cunt*, *fuck*, and even *arse*, but he still felt free to make blatant and repeated puns on them. Religious taboos were taking a much stronger hold than sexual ones. Most bodily functions were still plain everyday facts of life to be spoken about with practical simplicity. Even the translators of the King James' Bible were happy to use words like *piss*.

By the middle of the seventeenth century the Puritans were in power in England, but even then the principal concern was with religious taboos. Ancient terrors about the naming of supernatural beings were revived. The very name of God was avoided, as though by speaking it God himself might be invoked. This restriction echoed that of the Jews, who had believed for many centuries that except in certain very special circumstances it was wrong, even dangerous, to utter the name of God. Names for the Devil were likewise avoided.

Names of the powerful have always been regarded as powerful themselves. It is as though we are liable to confuse the name with the thing it represents. The idea is much the same as that underlying sympathetic magic. By manipulating a representation of something we think we might affect the thing itself.

It is for this reason that in many societies personal names are kept secret. Only immediate relatives know a person's 'real' name, everyone else uses a nickname. In ancient Greece certain priests abandoned their old names when they took up office, and it was illegal to address them by their old names rather than their new titles. For similar reasons new Christian names are given at baptism and confirmation. New names are also adopted by monks and nuns upon joining many religious orders. Bishops take the name of their See as a formal surname, and new popes also adopt new names. Their new names match their new lives, and break the power of their old ones.

In many Roman Catholic countries words associated with the Christian religion are still more strongly tabooed than those associated with sex or excretion. Even in English we still have a huge residue of religious swear-words. These are ancient oaths in which, for the most part, the offending name has been distorted beyond recognition. Many of them are now used only as meaningless exclamations.

After the restoration of the monarchy in England in 1660 puritanism declined sharply. Taboos of all kinds were thrown out of the window and liberalism flourished. By the middle of the eighteenth century, however, mores had started to change again. This time it was sex and excretion that were felt to need a clean up. Gentlemen took to using Latin terms so as not to offend delicate sensibilities. Authors like Edward Gibbon wrote their most interesting passages 'in the decent obscurity of a learned language'.

Soon after this the unsophisticated sensibilities of the newly powerful middle classes became paramount. It is no coincidence that the rise of prudery corresponded precisely with the rise of the bourgeoisie throughout the Western world. Prudery is the frigid bedfellow of philistinism.

In traditionally puritanical societies the prudes were firmly established by the early nineteenth century. It was the strait-laced United States, not, as is so often assumed, Victorian England, that perpetrated the silliest sexual evasions of the last century. Half-formed concepts of refinement led to the word *leg* being avoided since it denoted a supposedly indecent part of the anatomy. Not only human legs were thought indecent: chicken legs became *drumsticks*, and most other legs, including furniture legs, became *limbs*. So too, breasts (even chicken breasts) were called *bosoms*. Absurd as this may now sound, the effects are still with us. Rather than speak about chicken *legs* and *breasts*, as our eighteenth-century ancestors would have done without a second thought, some of us still use anodyne nineteenth-century terms like *white meat* and *dark meat*.

The strongest sexual taboos are associated with the genitals and sexual intercourse; but genital taboos arc so great that they affect other related matters. For example, clothing used to cover the genital region was not considered a proper topic of conversation until recently. Underwear and stockings were virtually unmentionable for over a century, and in 1907 a play by J. M. Synge, *The Playboy of the Western World*, broke up in disorder because the word *shift* was used. Even now words like *knickers* can elicit a nervous giggle from the especially prurient.

Verbal taboos carried over from the genitals affect not only underwear but also other regions of the body. So it is that *bellies* and *navels* are thought 'not quite nice'. Bodily characteristics which display sexual dimorphism are especially prone to taboo, although this is never as strong as that associated with the primary sexual organs. As secondary sexual characteristics the female breasts are only semi-taboo, and it is a few years now since Hollywood insisted that men should not expose their torsos on film unless their overtly masculine chest hair had been shaved off.

Along with sexual intercourse, a vast range of activity is tainted by its sexual nature. Included here are prostitution, adultery, masturbation, homosexuality, oral sex, and a range of other more imaginative pursuits.

To a lesser extent illness gives rise to its own taboos, so it is difficult to untangle taboos traditionally associated with both illness and sex. Suffice it to say that such matters are doubly stigmatized. Venereal disease for example suffers in this way. So do hernias. Menstruation, pregnancy and childbirth were regarded as types of feminine illness until surprisingly recently, and to some extent they are still stigmatized through their association with illness and sex. Women may still be heard speaking in lowered voices about 'little visitors', 'interesting conditions', and 'happy events'.

As gentlemen had taken to Latin, the ladies took to French. *Enceinte* was used in place of *pregnant* and giving birth was referred to as *accouchement*. An *arse* became a *derrière*. *Underwear* became *lingerie* (linen), and in particular the offensive *shift* became a *chemise*.

Excretion is the other main area in English currently affected by taboo. The main themes here are excrement itself, the act of depositing excrement, and places reserved for depositing it. There are, however, a number of bodily functions and products which fall into a related semi-taboo category. Farting, belching, and vomiting all belong here, as do sweat and snot. Suburban middle-class mothers still teach their daughters not to *sweat* ('pigs *sweat*, darling – ladies *perspire*'); and we all now employ the euphemism *handkerchief* where our ancestors would have referred plainly to a *wipe*, *muckinder*, or *snotter*.

Thomas Bowdler, an Edinburgh physician, brought out his expurgated version of Shakespeare's works in 1818. He also found it necessary to expurgate Gibbon's *Decline and Fall of the Roman Empire*, but even this paled in comparison with Noah Webster's efforts in the USA. In 1833 he brought out an expurgated version of the Bible.

London society was somewhat insulated against these bourgeois provincial tendencies. When Victoria came to the throne in 1837 it was, for example, still fashionable for ladies to wear dresses cut below the nipple.

Throughout their married life Queen Victoria and Prince Albert exchanged mildly erotic paintings of nudes. They and their circle thought little of it; only the servants disapproved. By the end of Victoria's reign, however, the position was different. The transatlantic tidal wave of illiberalism had swamped Britain; grotesque euphemism was in vogue, and plain speaking was illegal.

The anachronistic law of blasphemy attests to the strength of our primitive religious taboos, just as the laws of obscenity and indecency attest to the strength of taboos associated with sex and excretion. As George Orwell noted in *1984*, the scope of our thinking is to some extent dependent upon our vocabulary. At the back of the minds of would-be censors is the idea that if only we stopped using words with uncomfortable bodily associations then, perhaps, the things that they represent would go away. If we had no words for sex then we could not talk about it, and we would all lead clean, decent, upright, Christian lives. The idea is, of course, wildly unrealistic, but the lurking threat of thought control is not very attractive.

Fortunately, in this area at least, censorship is self-defeating. The stricter it is, the faster new euphemisms degenerate into obscenities. Furthermore, the power of taboo words becomes all the greater as attempts are made to ban them. It is a melancholy fact that names for the genitals have been used as terms of abuse only since prudery set in.

Insults such as *prick* and *fucking cunt* have come into existence as a direct result of the attitudes of the people whom they most offend.

Looking to the future, it is possible to foresee a number of areas which are likely to become taboo. Any subject for which we have developed a large number of euphemisms is a promising candidate. We already have dozens of them associated with insanity, money, and race. We have literally hundreds associated with drunkenness. Before the abolition of public executions we also had hundreds of euphemisms for hanging and the gallows. When executions were moved away from the public eye in the last century most of them fell into disuse. Now we have a similar number of euphemisms for death in general.

The subject of death has always been set about with euphemisms, their popularity fluctuating through the centuries as death became more or less taboo. Recently, there has been a noticeable shift towards the use of absurd and exaggerated euphemisms associated with the subject, which may indicate that the strength of death taboos are on the increase. The *dead* are the *deceased*, or the *dear departed*; they are said to have *passed away*, *fallen asleep*, or *gone to Jesus*.

The United States of America sets the pace in euphemism and genteelism, and it was there that the *funeral undertaker* first became a *mortician*, the *coffin* a *casket*, the *hearse* a *professional car* and the *graveyard* a *memorial park*. At the time of writing such expressions still sound preposterous, but within a few years they will probably seem perfectly reasonable. In the course of time the wheel may come full circle and the word *die* become unmentionable, as its counterpart was in Anglo-Saxon times.

It is not inconceivable that one day we shall face prosecution for using words like *grave*, *corpse* and *putrefaction*. If enough of us believe such words to be obscene, they surely will be.

James McDonald
January 1988

A NOTE ON SCOPE, SOURCES AND PRESENTATION

This book is eclectic rather than comprehensive. It deals, in alphabetical order, with some of the more important words associated with sex, excretion, and religion: the three areas most strongly stigmatized in English over the last thousand years. Terms associated with related matters such as 'bodily functions' are also included, but those associated with death and other quasi-taboo topics are not.

Most of the words dealt with are currently regarded as improper, or else are euphemisms for such words. Some were once regarded as improper, but have somehow managed to become respectable again. A few of special historical interest are included though they have fallen out of use in modern mainstream English. Others are included because of their etymologies, even though the words themselves are neither taboo nor euphemistic. These are words for which some dictionaries omit etymologies, or substitute misleading ones out of a misplaced sense of propriety.

It has been felt unnecessary to include details of the ordinary meanings of words as well as the meanings which are of immediate interest here. The analogies implicit in words such as *bagpipe*, *cherry*, *fig*, and *moon* generally speak for themselves. Only the principal obscene, taboo, and euphemistic meanings are dealt with. Also, the book is more concerned with historical development than current usage. Little emphasis is therefore given to the recent use of taboo words as insults.

In most cases head-words are not explicitly identified as verbs, nouns, or adjectives, since it is usually obvious to which category they belong. Where it is not obvious, or where the word can be used in more than one way, then each part of speech is identified explicitly.

Though most of the words included will be known throughout the English-speaking world, a few of them are peculiar to specific countries. These are mainly British, American and Australian, but they are all likely to become internationally known before too long.

Parallel terms from other major European languages are also given where they may be of interest.

Every effort has been made to avoid technical etymological detail, though the histories of words are given wherever possible. Whenever archaic spellings in quotations would be likely to confuse readers, the spellings have generally been modernized. On occasion, however, original spellings have been retained at the end of couplets to retain an intended rhyme. Where there is a danger of a word not being immediately understood it is explained in square brackets. For example the last two lines of one of the quotations at ARSE are given as:

> ... And he was ready with his iron hote [hot]
> And Nicholas amid the arse he smote.

Italics are used to draw attention to words and phrases being discussed, and capitals to indicate that the word is itself included as a head-word. Thus: 'The slang term *ass* is essentially the same word as *arse*, see ARSE', or combining the two conventions '*Ass* is essentially the same word as *ARSE*'.

Diacritics have generally been avoided, even in Anglo-Saxon and Latin words where it is customary to include macrons at least. Scholars who like such things can always fill them in themselves. Scholastic fashion prefers the expression 'Old English' to the traditional 'Anglo-Saxon', but 'Anglo-Saxon' is firmly embedded in the national consciousness and that is the term used throughout this book. It broadly includes English up to around 1150. 'Middle English' covers the period from 1150 to 1500, and 'Modern English' 1500 to the present day. Chaucer (1340?–1400) therefore wrote in Middle English and Shakespeare (1564–1616) in Modern English.

Wherever possible, quotations have been taken from well-known writers such as Chaucer and Shakespeare, rather than those such as Sir Thomas Urquhart, who specialized in scatology. For quotations from *The Canterbury Tales* references are given by group letter and line number. For quotations from Shakespeare's plays references are given to the name of the play, act number, scene number, and line number. (Line numbers may vary slightly in different editions of Shakespeare's works.)

Other principal sources include the King James' Bible of 1611 (also known as the Authorized Version), and the *Dictionary of the Vulgar Tongue*. The latter was compiled by one Captain Francis Grose and first published in 1785. Several revised editions appeared in the following fifty years, though most references in this book are to the one of 1811.

No attempt has been made to identify the strength of offence likely to be generated by each individual word. Concepts of obscenity and vulgarity are in any case a matter of personal taste. It is, however, relatively easy to distinguish between broadly acceptable and unacceptable words. Acceptable mainstream words are described as 'Standard English', and others as 'colloquial', abbreviated to 'col.' when given against a head-word. The few obsolete words included are similarly marked 'obs.'.

'*As politeness increases, some expressions will be considered as too gross and vulgar for the delicate . . .*'

Preface to Samuel Johnson's
A Dictionary of the English Language (1755)

A

ACORN

(col.) The head of an erect penis.

A term suggested by the similarity in appearance. This similarity is also recognized in the medical term for the head of the penis, *glans penis*, *glans* being the Latin word for an acorn.

Other colloquial terms for this part of the male anatomy include *BELL-END*, *helmet*, and *KNOB*, all of which also refer to visual similarities.

Long before the word *NUT* acquired its current slang meaning of testicle, it was also used as a term for the glans, again presumably because of the similarity in appearance.

ANUS

The arse hole, or as the Oxford English Dictionary puts it: 'The posterior opening of the alimentary canal in animals through which the excrements are ejected'.

The word was first used in English in the middle of the seventeenth century and has since displaced *arse* as the Standard English term. Like many of our genteelisms it is borrowed directly from Latin.

In Latin *anus* bears the double meaning of 'ring' and 'arse'. It therefore exactly parallels native English terms such as *RING*, *O*, *CIRCLE*, and *quoit*. From it we also have the word *anular* (sometimes spelled *annular*) meaning 'ring-shaped'.

Any term with excretary associations tends to become stigmatized, so even the word anus is avoided by many speakers. Indeed, the stigmatization extends to unconnected words such as *Uranus*, the traditional pronunciation of which is similar to 'your anus'. As a result some speakers, notably in the USA, have taken to pronouncing it something like 'ur-ahnus' or 'ur-arnus'.

ARSE

(col.) The anus or rump.

This is a venerable word with distinguished relatives throughout Europe, from Scandinavia to Greece.

In Anglo-Saxon times it was used as naturally as any other word, as it still is in a number of northern British dialects. In mainstream English, however, it has been regarded as impolite for several hundred years now.

Chaucer, writing in the fourteenth century, used the word freely in *The Canterbury Tales*. In the following passage, taken from *The Miller's Tale* (A 3731–40), the miller is relating Absolon's success, or lack of it in winning permission from Alison to give her a kiss. She is in her ground floor bedroom, he outside.

> . . . Dark was the night as pitch, or as coal
> And at the window out she put her hole
> And Absolon, he knew not bet nor worse
> But with his mouth he kissed her naked arse
> Full savourly, ere he was 'ware of this
> Aback he started, and thought it was amiss
> For well he knew a woman hath no beard
> He felt a thing all rough and long haired
> And said 'Fye! Alas! What have I do?'
> 'Tee-hee' quoth she, and clapped the window to . . .

Later (A 3798–810), Absolon comes back for his revenge, equipped with a red-hot poker. Nicholas, Alison's lover, is aware of what has happened and thinks that Absolon might be fooled again:

> This Nicholas had risen for to piss,
> And thought he would amend [improve] all the jape;
> He should kiss his arse ere that he 'scape.
> And up the window he did hastily,
> And out his arse he putteth prively
> Over the buttock, to the haunch-bone.
> And therewith spoke this clerk, this Absolon:
> 'Speak, sweet bird, I know not where thou art.'
> This Nicholas anon let flee a fart
> As great as it had been a thunder-dent [clap],
> That with the stroke he was almost yblent [blinded]

> And he was ready with his iron hote [hot]
> And Nicholas amid the arse he smote.

Nicholas's cries subsequently betrayed his adulterous liaison with Alison.

The next passage is also taken from *The Canterbury Tales*. During the telling of their stories the friar and the summoner take every opportunity to irritate each other. Here, in his prologue, the summoner is recounting a story about a friar who, in a vision, had been carried off to Hell. He is being shown around by a guide and has just asked why he can see no friars amongst the damned. In answer the guide addresses the Devil himself:

> . . . 'Hold up thy tail, thou Satan!' quoth he;
> 'shew forth thine arse, and let the Friar see
> where is the nest of friars in this place!'
> And ere that half a furlong way of space [i.e. very soon],
> Right so as bees out-swarm from a hive,
> Out of the Devil's arse there gone drive [i.e. rushed]
> Twenty thousand friars on a route,
> And throughout Hell swarmed all about,
> And came again as fast as they had gone
> And in his arse they crept – every one . . .

To express doubt or contempt we might say '*so is my arse*', just as our forefathers said '*so is mine arse*'; but we no longer say of a forgetful person that '*he would lose his arse if it were loose*': instead we use a more refined version with '*head*' replacing '*arse*'. So too, we now usually drop the last word in the seventeenth-century proverb about '*the pot calling the kettle black arse*'.

In the reign of Queen Anne there was a fashionable game at court which involved one person deceiving another into asking a question to which the first could answer 'my arse'. For example, a lady might enter a room in apparent distress crying 'It is white, and it follows me!' When asked what 'it' was she would reply in triumph 'my arse!'

The medlar, a type of apple eaten when very ripe, was traditionally known as an *open arse* because of its laxative properties. In one of Mercutio's bawdy speeches from *Romeo and Juliet* (II. i. 33–8) Shakespeare makes a pun on it as a term for the female genitals, but coyly writes it '*open et cætera*'; another type of fruit, the poperin pear, is used as an analogy for the male genitals:

3

If love be blind, love cannot hit the mark.
Now will he sit under a medlar tree,
And wish his mistress were that kind of fruit
As maids call medlars, when they laugh alone.

O Romeo! That she were, O! That she were
An open et cætera, thou a poperin pear ...

With reference to the medlar the *1811 Dictionary of the Vulgar Tongue* observes: 'it is never ripe till it is as rotten as a turd, and then it is not worth a fart'.

In the same dictionary under the heading 'Arse' we find the following colourful expression: 'He would lend his arse, and shit through his ribs; a saying of anyone who lends money inconsiderately.'

The bird now known as a *wheatear* does not have ears which in any way resemble wheat. In fact the '*wheat*' is a corruption of *white*, and when we remember that the Anglo-Saxon version of *arse* was *ears*, it is clear that the bird is really a 'white-arse'. Indeed, the bird does have a white rump, and in Cornish dialect it is known as a *whiteass*; in France it is called a *culblanc*, in Holland a *witstaat*, and in Germany a *weiss-schwanz*, all of which mean the same thing – 'white-tail' or 'white-arse'.

The great crested grebe and the little grebe were once known by the name '*arse-foot*', presumably because the legs of these birds are set unusually far back. It is no surprise therefore to find that the technical generic term for grebes, *podiceps*, is Latin for 'arse-footed'.

Ass

(col.) Rump or anus.

Although it is generally thought of as an American equivalent of the British *ARSE*, the pronunciation 'ass' also has a long history in the British Isles.

The word has provided a favourite pun for centuries, bearing as it does the dual meaning of rump and pack animal. Whenever Shakespeare mentions an ass (especially riding or sitting on one) the chances are that he expects his audience to think of *arse*.

AVOCADO

A pear shaped fruit.

Although the word has no sexual connotation in English, its origin might surprise a few maiden aunts.

The name is ultimately derived from an Aztec word for a testicle. The fruit apparently reminded the Aztecs of a scrotum containing a single testicle.

B

BAG

(col.) An old or unattractive woman.

This is a contraction of *baggage*, a word which has been used in much the same way since the seventeenth century.

In the sixteenth century the term *baggage* had, as well as its current meaning, a secondary one of 'military supplies'. From here the meaning was extended to female camp-followers who were also regarded as military supplies of a sort. This transfer of meaning was probably encouraged by a measure of confusion with the French word *bagasse* meaning prostitute.

BAGPIPE

(col.) To simulate sexual intercourse by inserting the penis into another's armpit.

The term, and therefore, presumably, the practice, has been around for centuries, but most dictionaries delicately omit to mention it.

Perhaps surprisingly this is not the only word in English for this practice: to *huffle* means exactly the same thing. Both *bagpipe* and *huffle* were included in the first *Dictionary of the Vulgar Tongue* (1785), but were omitted from later editions. Even in the 1785 edition the practice was described only as 'a piece of bestiality too filthy for explanation'.

BALLOCKS

(col.) Testicles.

Essentially the same word as *BOLLOCKS*, this is actually the earlier form. Its spelling reflects the close etymological connection with the word *ball* (see BALLS).

Once Standard English, the word is now considered impolite, even offensive in certain quarters.

The *Oxford English Dictionary* gives examples of the word's use from around AD 1000. Here is one from the middle of the fifteenth century 'I have brysten both my balok stones, so fast hyed I hedyer' ('I have burst both my ballock-stones, so fast hied I hither'). Ballock breaking effort is nothing new.

For no very obvious reason parsons were, for hundreds of years up to the last century, popularly called *Ballocks*, a convenient fact which has provided a successful defence in at least one obscenity trial in this century.

Ballocky Bill the Sailor was the name of a generously testicled fictional character celebrated in verse in the nineteenth century. His doings are still recounted by rugby players, but his name is often unaccountably changed to *Barnacle Bill the Sailor*.

BALLS

(col.) Testicles; also nonsense, as in 'talking a load of balls'. *A balls up is a mess, and* to ball *is to have sexual intercourse.*

The use of the word balls for testicles is clearly suggested by their approximately spherical shape. Similar metaphors include *MARBLES*, *BILLIARDS*, *GOOLIES*, *NUTS*, and *PILLS*. Indeed the traditional English word for testicles, *STONES*, was presumably adopted for similar reasons, as were the more recent colloquial terms, *pebbles* and *rocks*.

As a verb meaning to copulate the expression *to ball* seems to have come into common usage only in the second half of the twentieth century. Shakespeare's meaning in *Henry VIII* (II. iii. 44–8) is questionable:

ANNE. . . . I swear again, I would not be a queen
  For all the world.

OLD LADY. In faith, for little England
You'd venture an emballing: I myself
Would for Carnarvenshire . . .

Here, *emballing* ostensibly refers to the orb used at royal investitures, but it is tempting to imagine a deliberate pun.

BANG

(col.) A synonym for fuck, both as noun and verb.

This is one of many words for sexual intercourse with associations of violence (see BONK).

The meaning is not as recent as might be thought: in the early eighteenth century, for example, prostitutes were sometimes known as *bang-tails*.

To bang like a shit house door in a gale appears to be an adaptation of the original Australian *to bang like a dunny door in a gale*. Both expressions mean 'to copulate with enthusiasm and vigour'.

See also GANG BANG.

BASKET

(col.) Bastard (UK), Crotch (USA).

In Britain the word is an old euphemism making a simple play upon the similarity in sound between *bastard* and *basket*. In earlier centuries illicit sexual intercourse was known as *basket-making*.

In the USA the term can be used to describe male genitalia, the outline of which can be seen through the clothing. Hence, a *basket-watcher* is one given to looking at male crotches, and to have a *basket lunch* is to perform impromptu fellatio.

BASTARD

An illegitimate child.

Outside its neutral legal use, this word is still used as an insult, despite the fact that illegitimacy is now supposed to have lost its Victorian stigma.

In much earlier times there was no great shame about bastardy in Europe. The man now known as *William the Conqueror* or *William I*, was, in more robust times, called *William the Bastard* or simply *William Bastard*. There are families to this day who are proud to bear the surname *Bastard*.

In Old French the word *bast* denoted a pack saddle, as does its modern French descendant *bât*, the circumflex marking the old atrophied *s*. Pack saddles were used to make up improvised beds by men on the move. If they shared their temporary bed with local women, as they were wont to do, the consequence might well have been a bastard, hence the name.

What we call a bastard and the French call a *bâtard*, the Germans call a *bänkling*, literally a child conceived upon a bank or bench. This probably explains the origin of the English word *bankling*, which also denotes an illegitimate child.

BAWD

A procuress or, occasionally, a pimp.

The word has been used in English for centuries, having been adapted from the Old French *baude*, a term with exactly the same meaning.

Traditional euphemisms for bawds include *madam*, *aunt*, *mother*, *dame*, *abbess* (see NUNNERY), and *buttock broker*.

BAZOOMAS

(col.) The female breasts.

Presumably the word is a corruption of *bosoms*.

It belongs to a comprehensive range of humorous expressions for mammary apparatus. Other examples are *bejonkers*, *baloobas*, *bazonkers*, *balloons*, *bouncers*, *bumpers*, *diddies*, *melons*, *udders*, *upholstery*, *dairies*, *boobs*, *boobies*, *bubbies*, and *jugs*.

BEARD

(col.) Female pubic hair.

An ancient euphemism employing obvious imagery.

Since at least the seventeenth century the term *beard-splitter* has been used for men who frequent prostitutes. Similar old expressions include *hair-splitter*, *hair-divider*, and *beard-jammer*.

An Australian expression for sexual intercourse which recently enjoyed a few years of popularity was '*to spear the bearded clam*'. Another Australian expression which has gained international currency is *to don the beard*, meaning to perform cunnilingus.

BEAVER

(col.) The female genitals.

Popular in the USA, this expression has no convincing etymology. The most likely theory is that it is a contraction of *beaver tail* (see TAIL), but it may be significant that a certain type of beard is known as a *beaver* (see BEARD).

BELL

(col.) The clitoris.

Having originated in the USA this term has now gained international currency.

Although most people appreciate that there is some sexual connotation to the word, many are apparently not sure exactly what it is. Songs such as Anita Ward's 'Ring My Bell' would almost certainly have been banned by the BBC had the nature of the subject-matter been fully appreciated.

BELL-END

(col.) The penis end.

The expression refers to a fancied resemblance in appearance (see ACORN). For added vividness a *bell-end* is sometimes called a *cheesy bell-end*.

BELLY

What the educated call an abdomen, *the uneducated a* stomach, *and the puerile a* tummy.

Belly is a good practical word of Anglo–Saxon derivation which is being edged out of use by the over-sensitive.

It is closely related to *bellows*: their common ancestor being a Saxon word for a bag.

BERK

(col.) A foolish person.

Many who use this word might be surprised, and perhaps shocked, by its original meaning.

The term is a contraction of *Berkshire Hunt* or *Berkeley Hunt*: in either case it is Cockney rhyming slang for *CUNT* (see also JOEY and CHARLIE).

BIDET

A basin used for washing the genital and anal areas.

This is an unusual word in that it was once regarded as vulgar but has now regained respectability.

The *1811 Dictionary of the Vulgar Tongue* gives a coy description along with an accurate etymology: 'A kind of tub, contrived for ladies to wash themselves, for which purpose they bestride it like a French poney, or post-horse, called in French bidets.'

BILLIARDS

(col.) Testicles. Hence to play billiards *meaning to fondle or play with the testicles.*

In modern usage it is most often encountered in the expression *pocket billiards*, but the analogy has been around for centuries. In *Anthony and Cleopatra* (II. iii. 3–9) Shakespeare has Cleopatra anachronistically ask a man to join her for a game of billiards, pointing out that as a partner another woman would be no more use than a eunuch.

The metaphor is much the same as that implicit in the use of the word *BALL* for 'testicle'.

BIRD

(*col.*) *A young woman.*

The word has been in use in this sense since the Middle Ages. Originally it could be used for any young animal. Even amongst feathered animals only nestlings and fledgelings were known as *birds* – when they grew up they were called *fowl*.

As the supplement to the *Oxford English Dictionary* notes, the term is often used familiarly or disparagingly (see BITCH). It is certainly not a favourite amongst feminists.

The expression *to do bird* is unconnected. It is Cockney rhyming slang, the full form being *to do bird lime*: to do time (in prison).

BITCH

(*col.*) *A lewd or spiteful woman.*

A clearly uncomplimentary term, it has been in continual use since at least AD 1400.

It is one of many names for female animals which have been opprobriously transferred to women. Other well-known examples are *COW*, *SOW*, *CAT*, *shrew*, and *cattle*. Less offensive are *doe*, *filly*, *BIRD*, *hen*, and *chick*. It is curious that while a *foxy* woman is sexy, a *vixen* is thoroughly undesirable; and although the adjective *shrewd* (i.e. 'shrew-like') is complimentary, its twin *shrewish* is certainly not.

For animal names applied to men see BULL.

There is a long history in English of words for women being devalued and becoming offensive. This systematic denigration of women is reflected, for example, in the history of words such as *HUSSY*, *NYMPH*, *MISTRESS*, *TART*, and *WHORE*. Why this should happen so consistently is something of a mystery, but whatever the reason the language is already littered by dozens, even hundreds, of such devalued words.

See also SON OF A BITCH.

BLETHERSKATE

A Scottish term of abuse; also found in the USA where it is generally spelled blatherskite.

The etymology of the word is apparent when it is split up into its constituent elements – *blether/blather* and *skate/skite*. *Blether/blather* is essentially the same as *bladder*, originally meaning simply a bag, and *skate/skite* is a northern dialect form of *shite*. A *bletherskate*, then, is literally a 'bag of shit'.

One reason why the word established itself in the USA is that it features in the Scots song 'Maggie Lauder', which was popular amongst the revolutionaries during the American War of Independence. The relevant line is: 'Jog on your gait, ye blatherskate'.

BLIMEY

(*col.*) See GOR BLIMEY.

BLOODY

(*col.*) *An entirely meaningless adjective used for emphasis.*

For no very good reason this word is popularly considered to be a swear-word, and has been so considered for three or four hundred years. In some quarters it is thought so offensive that it has to be replaced by disguised oaths such as *ruddy* and *bally*. (See SWEAR-WORD.)

One explanation of the word's origin associates it with 'blood' in the old sense of disreputable aristocrat. *Bloody* behaviour would be that appropriate to young bloods – objectionable and profane. An alternative explanation relies upon the extension of literal expressions such as *bloody war*, *bloody butcher*, and *bloody massacre*.

There is absolutely no evidence to support the story that the word is a corruption of the phrase 'By Our Lady', an oath calling upon supernatural assistance from the Virgin Mary.

BLOOMERS

Women's baggy knickers.

Although it is no longer as risqué as it once was, the word still retains a slightly humorous flavour from the time when any mention of underclothes was rather daring. Even today popular comedians can extract a laugh from especially vacuous audiences by the mere mention of bloomers.

Bloomers were originally not underclothes at all, but baggy trousers intended to be worn by women as part of a costume similar to that traditionally used by Turkish women.

The name came from that of *Mrs Amelia Bloomer*, a pioneer of women's rights in the USA during the nineteenth century, who advocated the use of such clothing.

BOG

(col.) A lavatory.

As so often, Shakespeare was apparently the first to record the word with this meaning. In *The Comedy of Errors* (III. ii. 114–16) two characters are likening parts of a woman's body to various countries. The traditional association between Ireland and bogs provides the double entendre:

> ANTIPHOLUS OF SYRACUSE. In what part of her body stands Ireland?
> DROMIO OF SYRACUSE. Marry, sir, in her buttocks: I found it out by the bogs.

As an explicit contraction of *bog house* the term was in use in the early eighteen hundreds at Oxford University, and has since gained international popularity.

For various synonyms see LAVATORY.

BOLLOCKS

(col.) Testicles.

This is a modern form of an ancient word usually spelt *BAL-LOCKS*. It was Standard English up until the early nineteenth century, but is now regarded as colloquial.

BONK

(*col.*) *A synonym for fuck, both as noun and verb.*

Popular only since the early 1980s, this term may have been suggested by the expression '*to have a bonk on*', meaning to have an erection, a phrase which dates back to the 1950s.

Especially popular among the young, this word has joined a large family of sexual terms which are also associated with violence. Other such terms are *BANG* and *WHAM-BANG*, *KNOCK* (*up* or *off*), *GRIND*, *bump*, *hit*, *beat*, *hammer*, *ream*, *SCREW*, *clap*, *cope*, *strike*, and *thump*. For yet more examples see WEAPON.

Violent words are used for sexual intercourse in many European languages. Well-known examples are the German *bumsen* and *ficken*, and the French *baiser* and *foutre*.

BOTTLE

(*col.*) *Arse.*

This is an example of Cockney rhyming slang, the full form being *bottle and glass* – not a very good rhyme in some forms of English, though, of course, it is in traditional Cockney speech.

To lose one's bottle is *to lose one's arse*, or more precisely to lose control of one's anal sphyncter muscle, a common symptom of extreme fear. The same phenomenon is referred to in expressions such as *to be shit scared* and *to fill one's pants*.

By extension the word *bottle* has acquired a secondary meaning of 'courage'. To have *a lot of bottle* is to have a lot of courage, and to *bottle-out* is to fail through cowardice.

BOX

(*col.*) *The vagina.*

Often assumed to be American in origin, this use of the word turns out to have a long history in England. In *All's Well that Ends Well* (II. iii. 282–4) Shakespeare uses the word fairly explicitly:

> . . . He wears his honour in a box unseen,
> That hugs his kicky-wicky [penis] here at home,
> Spending his manly marrow in her arms . . .

Nowadays, when used in this sense, the word is often found in compounds such as *jelly box*, and *dirt box* (this unattractive latter term being borrowed from the world of engineering).

BRASS NAIL

(*col.*) *A prostitute.*

This is Cockney rhyming slang, the missing rhyme being provided by the word *TAIL*, a colloquial term for a prostitute.

BREAST

The chest area of any animal, also the mammary appurtenances found there in female mammals.

A neutral enough word, one might have thought. Yet even this was too much for prudes in the last century, especially in the USA:

> Fate had placed me opposite a fine turkey. I asked my partner if I should have the pleasure of helping her to a piece of the breast. She looked at me indignantly, and said, 'Curse your impudence, sar; I wonder where you larn manners. Sar, I take a lilly turkey bosom, if you please'. ('Peter Simple'[2])

Other evasions include *chest*, *bust*, *contours*, *charms*, *upper regions*, and *frontal development*.

Until recent years the BBC allowed broadcasters to use the word only in the singular. *The breast* was acceptable, but *breasts* were not.

BRISTOLS

(*col.*) *The female breasts.*

This is another example of opaque Cockney rhyming slang. The full form is *Bristol Cities*, rhyming with *titties*.

---

[2] *Peter Simple*, ch. 31, quoted by Earnest Weekly in *The Romance of Words* (see Bibliography) ch. 7.

BROTHEL

A bawdy house.

The original Anglo-Saxon version of this word denoted not a building but a ruined man. In the Middle Ages there seems to have been some confusion between the expressions *brothel's house* and *bordel house* ('bordello'). This mix-up produced the hybrid *brothel house* and thence *brothel*.

The English language harbours dozens of alternative names for brothels Some of the more picturesque are *NUNNERY, academy, school of Venus, vaulting school, cat house, buttocking shop*, and *knocking shop*.

BROWN EYE

(col.) Anus.

To chuck a brown eye is to expose one's anus, a slight embellishment of the more traditional practice of mooning.

For centuries the word *eye* has been used as a euphemism for the anus or the female genitals. The female genitals are also sometimes called a *long-eye*.

BUGGER

As a noun, a sodomite; as a verb, to engage in sodomy.

Derived from the Latin *Bulgarus*, meaning 'Bulgarian', this word was originally applied to a group of Bulgarian heretics who were falsely accused of sodomy in the Middle Ages. The spurious charge of sodomy is one of the traditional libels applied by the Roman Catholic Church to those who question its dogmas.

The word is used as a legal term, although in this context it covers bestiality as well as sodomy. Bestiality is sexual congress with an animal, and as policemen are reminded in Calvert's *Powers of Arrest and Charges*:[3]

[3] Fred Calvert, *The Constable's Pocket Guide to Powers of Arrest and Charges*, 7th Edn, p. 25 (1982).

... the expression 'animal' includes fish (e.g. skate, etc.) and fowl (e.g. turkey, etc.) for the purpose of this crime ...

In keeping with the word's earliest use it is still used as a general term of abuse, and in recent times also as an exclamation. To dilute any impropriety it is often amended to '*beggar*', as in the sympathetic '*poor beggar!*'.

BULL

(*col.*) *A sexually renowned man, also nonsense as in* a load of bull.

The term is one of many names for male animals applied to men which carry connotations of sexual ability. Other well-known examples are *ram*, *boar*, *buck*, *stag*, *STALLION*, and *stud*. In nineteenth-century America these words were considered positively indecent, and were avoided by those with pretensions to good breeding. Amazing as it now seems, bulls were then known by names such as *cow creature* and *gentleman cow*.

In previous centuries men were also likened to monkeys, goats, and mules for much the same reason, all of these animals having a reputation for concupiscence. Less complimentary are (*old*) *fox*, and (*a bit of a*) *dog*; and less complimentary still *wolf* and *lounge lizard*. For animal names applied to women see BITCH.

Bulls have always been known for their sexual proclivities, a fact which may account for the very name. It has been suggested that the ancient Proto-Indo-European forerunner of the word *bull* meant 'the impregnater'.

Bull is also occasionally used as a verb, as, for example, in the seventeenth-century proverb *who bulls the cow must keep the calf*.

Bull dicker and *bull dyke* are terms applied to especially masculine lesbians.

As a synonym for nonsense, *bull* is not a contraction of *bull-shit* as is often assumed. *Bull-shit* was a later extension of the earlier *bull*. The original reference was probably to a *papal bull*, a formal document sealed with a *bulla*: such documents having traditionally been regarded with a measure of scepticism in Protestant countries.

BUM

(col.) Rump, arse.

This word came into popular usage in the late Middle Ages, around the same time that *ARSE* started to become regarded as improper.

Shakespeare used the word quite freely. In *Measure for Measure* (II. i. 218), for example: 'Your bum is the greatest thing about you'.

Ultimately the word is related to *boom*, bums being responsible for booms, i.e. flatulence. The theory that *bum* is an abbreviation of *bottom* is untenable, since *bottom* was not used in this sense until the eighteenth century.

The word appears in numerous compounds: first recorded in the sixteenth century, a *bum card* is a marked playing card, a *bum boy* is a catamite, a *bum shop* is a brothel, and a *bum sucker* is a toady. At Oxford University a short commoner's gown is called a *bum curtain*, and, when such things were popular, bustles were generally known as *bum-rolls*. See also BUMF, BUMJUMPER, and BUM-TAGS.

Even in the early nineteenth century the word was still in the process of displacing the more traditional *arse*. The *1811 Dictionary of the Vulgar Tongue* relates a story of a woman who insisted on calling a jack ass a '*johnny bum*'. She would not say *jack* because it was vulgar, nor *ass* because it was indecent.

To want to know the ins and outs of a duck's bum is to want to know all the trivial details about the business of others.

The word *bummer*, denoting any bad experience, is at least a hundred years old. It was originally a horse racing term and referred specifically to heavy betting losses. In this context a *bum* was a sponger or tramp, as in current American usage.

BUMF

(col.) Paper, especially that conventionally shuffled by bureau-crats.

This is an abbreviation of *bum-fodder*, an old term for what we now know as lavatory paper.

From 1650 or so up until the nineteenth century, *bum-fodder* was the Standard English expression for cheap and trashy literature.

The French *torche-cul* is an exact counterpart. It retains both meanings 'lavatory paper' and 'cheap literature'. At one time it was also used in England with the meaning of 'lavatory paper'.

BUMTAGS

(*col.*) *Bits of excrement sticking to the hair around the anus.*

This is one of numerous words with the same meaning (see CLINKERS).

BUSH

(*col.*) *The female pubic hair.*

In the middle of the last century this was still a delicate literary euphemism, but since then it has become an everyday colloquialism.

It echoes other bucolic metaphors such as *undergrowth*, *ling*, *thicket*, *garden* and *flower*, all of which have been used in the same way for many centuries. A similar idea lies behind the word *deflower* meaning 'devirginate', and the more thorough-going term *defoliate*.

The Romans referred to the female pubic hair as a 'fern', and the Greeks as a 'rose bush'.

BUSINESS

Shit.

This is a blatant euphemism. It is most often found in the expression '*to do one's business*'. This expression is so well known that it seems to have been necessary to doctor Psalm 107. In the King James' Bible verse 23 refers to 'They ... that do business in great waters' but the Book of Common Prayer prefers 'They ... that occupy their business in great waters'.

Other euphemisms comparable in their evasiveness include *do one's duty*, *take the dog for a walk*, and *powder one's nose*.

BUTTOCKS

The rump.

The word is derived from *butt*, a term which was itself once Standard English for the rump and which is still in common use in the USA. In more general usage the word *butt* may be applied to the blunt end of any object.

In previous centuries the word *buttock* was used as a name for a prostitute. Thus a *buttock broker* was a procurer, *buttock broking* was harlotry, a *buttock ball* was a dance attended by prostitutes, and a *buttock shop* was a brothel.

C

CACK

(col.) As a noun, excrement; as a verb, to excrete.

In its use as both noun and verb it resembles many other terms concerning the same subject, for example *shit*, *crap*, and *dung*.

It is an ancient word with relatives throughout Europe and beyond. Our modern form seems to come from the Dutch, but it is recognizably related to the Latin *cacare*. In other languages it appears as *kakkan* (Greek), *kakat* (Russian), *kakati* (Czech), *cacaim* (Irish), and *kuka* (Icelandic). Ultimately it probably derives from a child's echoic word sounding something like *ka-ka*.

Although most often found in dialect now, it does still occur in mainstream English. The common term *cack-handed* for example, meaning left-handed, reflects an ancient disapproval of left-handedness, and possibly the practice of using the right hand for eating and the left for assisting with excretory functions. Like many terms denoting left-handedness, *cack-handed* has also acquired a further meaning of 'uncoordinated' or 'clumsy'.

In parts of northern England the expression *cacking down* is used in much the same way as the more widespread *pissing down* – to signify heavy rainfall.

The word also occurs in *cacafuego*, literally 'shit-fire', an expression applied to particularly vocal braggarts, and in heavily distorted forms it also features in *POPPYCOCK* and less obviously in *DUCKING STOOL*.

Cat

(*col.*) *A spiteful woman. Also a homosexual man.*

The two meanings correspond to quite distinct words.

The first refers to the animal, and is one of the many animal names applied to women (see BITCH). Brothels are sometimes known as *cat houses*.

The second is an abbreviation of the word *catamite* which more accurately denotes a boy kept by a man for immoral purposes. *Catamite* is itself an unlikely Latin corruption of the Greek name *Ganymede*; the original Ganymede being not only cup bearer to the gods but also Zeus's catamite.

Catamite

See CAT.

Charlie, also Charley

(*col.*) *A fool, especially in the phrase* a right charlie.

This is a contraction of *Charlie Hunt*, Cockney rhyming slang for *cunt*. See also BERK and JOEY, both of which have similar derivations.

Cherry

(*col.*) *The hymen, hence figuratively virginity.*

This is primarily an American term, the details of the loss of one's cherry being a favourite topic of conversation in the USA.

Chopper

(*col.*) *The penis.*

Although apparently coined only in this century the term has already gained wide currency. It is one of many names for the penis associated with violence (see WEAPON).

Chunder

(*col.*) *To vomit.*

Although Australian in origin, this term now supplements the inter-nationally-known stock of names for this activity. Conventional alternatives include *puke*, *retch*, *spew*, *heave*, *honk*, *york*, *chuck up*, *throw up*, *be sick*, and in the USA *barf*.

Although words for vomiting are not regarded as truly taboo, they are nevertheless generally avoided in polite conversation. The fact that there are so many alternative terms for vomiting is itself an indication that the subject matter is thought indelicate. As a general rule the more terms there are for an object or activity the less socially acceptable it is.

The development of numerous euphemisms with humorous overtones suggests that the conventional terms are coming to be increasingly avoided, and may in time come to be regarded as objectionable. Recent humorous euphemisms include *calling Hughie* or *Ruth* or *Ralph*, having a *technicolour yawn*, and *talking down the great white telephone* [i.e. lavatory basin]. The expression *to flash the hash*, however, is not as recent as is often assumed; it dates at least as far back as the eighteenth century.

Circle

(*col.*) *The vagina.*

One of a number of terms referring to the real or imagined shape of this part of the female anatomy. Similar metaphors are *RING*, *hoop*, *doughnut*, *HOLE*, and *horse collar*. Except for *horse collar*, these metaphors are also applied to the anus.

Shakespeare provides an early example of the word as used in the sense of 'vagina'. In *Romeo and Juliet* (II. i. 23–7) Mercutio, speaking of Romeo, says:

> ... 'twould anger him
> To raise a spirit in his mistress' circle
> Of some strange nature, letting it there stand
> Till she had laid it, and conjured it down ...

The context of the speech (Mercutio has just been talking about the demesnes adjacent to Rosalind's quivering thigh) makes it clear that a double entendre is intended.

In more recent times the expression *vicious circle* has provided many less inspired punsters with the raw material for similar jokes.

CLAP

(col.) Venereal disease, specifically gonorrhoea.

The term dates from the sixteenth century, having been adapted from the French *clapoir*, which denoted a bubo or swelling in the groin. Such swellings are symptomatic of gonorrhoea.

CLINKERS

(col.) Pieces of faecal matter sticking in the hair around the anus.

This word has been current in the UK since at least the 1830s, but is now more popular in Australia. (See also DILBERRIES.)

CLIT

(col.) The clitoris.

An abbreviation of the Standard English *clitoris*, the word is also sometimes used as a term of abuse.

Clitoris is unusual in that it is borrowed directly from Greek. We usually rely on Latin for our formal words to do with sex.

Other familiar terms for this part of the anatomy include *BELL*, *button*, *dot*, and *little man* (see LITTLE MAN IN A BOAT). Another alternative, borrowed from the French, is *praline*. Literally it denotes a sugared almond, an object which, at least in appearance, the clitoris is thought to resemble.

COBBLERS

(col.) Testicles, also nonsense.

This is another example of Cockney rhyming slang. The full form is *cobbler's awls*; an awl being an instrument used in leather working.

The missing rhyme is provided by the word *balls* with its dual meaning of 'testicles' and 'nonsense'. A *load of cobblers* is a load of balls in the sense of a 'load of rubbish'.

Many of those who use the phrase do not recognize it as a synonym for *balls*. Indeed, most people who use it do not even realize that it is rhyming slang at all.

See also ORCHESTRAS.

Cock

(col.) The penis.

This was Standard English for centuries, but is now regarded as improper.

The word was originally used in ancient times as the name for certain fowl – as indeed it still is. Apparently because of the resemblance in appearance between a chicken's neck and a water tap, the name *water cock* was given to taps in the Middle Ages. We still use the word in the sense when we talk of *stop cocks* and *sea cocks*. Then the resemblance between a water tap and a penis, in both shape and function, suggested the use of the word for a penis as well.

North America with its puritanical traditions did not like such associations, a fact which largely explains why, even to this day, water cocks are called *faucets* and cockerels are called *roosters* in the USA. At one time some Americans even referred to cockswains as '*rooster-swains*'.

A number of derivative expressions are widely used. Typical examples are *Cock Inn* meaning vagina, but punning on a traditional pub name; *cock-smitten* and *cockish*, both used of women unduly enamoured of men; *cock-teaser*, applied to a woman who leads a man on; and *cock-tax*, an Australian term for alimony.

Cod

The scrotum.

Occasionally the word is used to mean testicle, but this seems to stem from a misunderstanding about its traditional usage.

As so often occurs, our supposedly respectable Latin word for this part of the anatomy originally meant exactly the same as the native English one it replaced. Both *scrotum* and *cod* simply mean 'bag'.

Since Anglo–Saxon times *cod* has been used for various types of bag or pod. For example a *pease-cod* is an alternative name for what we now generally call a *pea pod*. So too the term *cod-end* is used to denote the bag-like end of a fishing net. (The net is not named after the fish called *cod* – if anything it was the other way round.)

The word is now best known from the term *codpiece*, the name of the bag-like flap traditionally worn at the genital area of breeches or hose.

In *Love's Labour's Lost* (III. i. 181) Cupid is called the 'King of codpieces', and in *Much Ado About Nothing* (III. iii. 133) the word is used euphemistically when Hercules' codpiece is described as being as massy as his club.

COME

(*col.*) *As a noun, semen; as a verb, to ejaculate.*

Shakespeare was probably one of the first to record this meaning. Here is an example from *Troilus and Cressida* (IV. ii. 36–9):

CRESSIDA. . . . My lord, come you again into my chamber:
    You smile and mock me, as if I meant naughtily.
TROILUS. Ha, ha!
CRESSIDA. Come, you are deceived, I think of no such thing.

In *Bishop Percey's Loose Songs*, written around 1650, we find the word used more explicitly:

> . . . Then off he came,
> & blusht for shame
> Soe soone that he had endit.

COMMODITY

(*col.*) *The vagina.*

As the *1811 Dictionary of the Vulgar Tongue* put it: '. . . the private parts of a modest woman, and the public parts of a prostitute'.

Once popular, the term is now quite rare, though not obsolete.

Con

(col.) Vagina.

This is the French equivalent of the native English *CUNT*, although it is not certain how closely the words are related.

Con is derived from the Latin word for the female genitals, *cunnus*, which evolved from *cuneus*, the Latin word for a wedge. The connection is the patch of female pubic hair, which is wedge-shaped. Also from the Latin is the English word *cuneiform* which means 'wedge-shaped': cuneiform writing for example is the ancient type of writing formed by impressing wedge-shaped reed ends into wet clay.

For centuries *con* has created trouble by being confused with various similar English words. Here, from Shakespeare's *Henry V* (III. ii. 47–53), is an example where it is being confused with the word *gown*, which Alice mispronounces *coun* (*foot* is also being confused with *foutre*, the French counterpart of *FUCK*):

KATHERINE. . . . Comment appelez vous le pied et la robe?
ALICE. Le foot, madam; et le coun.
KATHERINE. Le foot, et le coun? O Seigneur Dieu! ils sont les mots de mauvais corruptible, gros, et impudique, et non pour les dames d'honneur d'user. Je ne voudrais prononcer ces mots devant les seigneurs de France pour tout le monde. Foh! le foot et le coun.

For other such puns see CONSTABLE.

Condom

A contraceptive sheath.

Originally spelled *cundum*, the word is several hundred years old. According to the supplement to the *Oxford English Dictionary* its origin is unknown, although other authorities assert that it was adopted from the name of one of the great proponents of the contraceptive sheath, Colonel Cundum, a British Guards officer in the seventeenth century.

Certainly the idea of using a sheath for contraception predates the introduction of suitable rubber. Giacomo Casanova, for one, tested animal intestines for this purpose.

Condoms are also popularly known as *rubber johnnies* (see JOHNNEY), and *French letters* (see FRENCH SICKNESS).

Internationally, colloquial terms for condoms are liable to cause a range of misunderstandings, even within the English-speaking world. An Australian, for example, may refer to a *frangler* which will mean nothing at all to a Briton. On the other hand, the Australian will use the word *durex* to mean stickytape: in Australia *Durex* is a trade name for such tape, not for contraceptive sheaths as it is in Britain.

In the USA condoms are called *rubbers*. To an American the device used to rub out pencil marks is called an *eraser*, so Britons asking for a rubber run the risk of a serious misunderstanding.

As a final complication the trade name *XXXX* is used in Australia and the UK for a brand of lager, but in the USA for a brand of condom.

CONSTABLE

(obs. col.) The vagina.

This meaning is based upon a pun, the first syllable resembling both the French *CON* and the English *CUNT*. Here is an example of Shakespeare using it in *All's Well That Ends Well* (II. ii. 29–34) where we have already learned that the clown's 'answer' will suit a number of bawdy purposes:

COUNTESS. Have you, I say, an answer of such fitness for all questions?
CLOWN. From beneath your duke to beneath your constable, it will fit any question.
COUNTESS. It must be an answer of most monstrous size that must fit all demands.

By the late eighteenth century the pun was so rife, and mores so delicate, that some people were driven to use the word *thingstable* instead of *constable* in their everyday speech.

Things are not quite so bad today but the pun is still widely recognized. For example there are a number of suggestive songs in which the word *cunt* at the end of one line is lost in *constable*, the first word of the next.

CONVENIENCE
See LAVATORY.

COPULATE

To have sexual intercourse.

The word is fashioned after the Latin verb *copulare*, meaning to bind, fasten, or couple. Like many Latin terms with sexual associations it has been in use in English for centuries.

Originally such words were primarily used amongst classically educated gentlemen to discuss matters which they did not want ladies, children, or the lower orders to know about.

COR BLIMEY!

(col.) See GOR BLIMEY!

COUNTRY

A word full of possibilities for punning with cunt.

Shakespeare used the pun often, although his usage was more euphemistic than humorous. In the following exchange from *Hamlet* (III. ii. 116–22) Hamlet and Ophelia are having a slight misunderstanding, made possible by the use of the word lap, which in Shakespeare's time could mean something more intimate than it does to us:

> HAMLET. Lady, shall I lie in your lap?
> OPHELIA. No, my lord.
> HAMLET. I mean my head upon your lap?
> OPHELIA. Aye, my lord.
> HAMLET. Do you think I meant country matters?
> OPHELIA. I think nothing, my lord.
> HAMLET. That's a fair thought to lie between maids' legs.

Throughout his works Shakespeare often extends the pun to specific countries. References to the *Low Countries* and the *Netherlands* are almost invariably sexual, and *Holland* ('hole-land', the anus) provides endless potential (see BOGS for a further example).

Unwearied by age, the *country–cunt* pun continues to amuse. For each new generation of children the following lines

> I'll fight for my cunt,
> I'll fight for my cunt,
> I'll fight for my cunt-er-ee

will no doubt continue to appear original, as they have done for untold years already.

COVER

(col.) To copulate.

The word is Standard English for copulation between animals, especially large animals. The male is said to cover the female.

Shakespeare used the word in *Othello* (i. i. 113) 'you'll have your daughter covered with a Barbary horse . . .'.

For similar rural terms for copulation adopted for use among humans see TUP.

COW

(col.) An unpleasant woman.

This is one of many derogatory terms likening women to female animals (see BITCH).

It is slightly less offensive when used to mean specifically 'wife' since this is Cockney rhyming slang, the full form being *cow and kisses* – 'missis'.

In the 1960s the term was regarded as too offensive for use on television. Johnny Speight therefore invented the evasive term *moo*, as in the now well-known phrase '*silly old moo*', for use in the programme 'Till Death Us Do Part'. It soon caught on, and still enjoys considerable popularity.

CRACK

(*col.*) *The vagina, also a woman regarded as a sex object.*

This is one of many terms referring to the cleft of the external female genitals. Others are *breach, chink, cranny, crease, gap, GASH, nick, nook, notch, SLIT, vent,* and *wound.*

It has also been used as a synonym for *prostitute* since at least the seventeenth century.

CRAP

(*col.*) *As a noun, excrement; as a verb, to excrete.*

Although the word itself is very old, this particular meaning seems to be relatively recent, no occurrences having been recorded before the mid nineteenth century. Before then the word *crap* had had a number of meanings all associated with rejected material, rubbish, dregs, or dirt. The extension to excrement would not, therefore, be difficult. In fact the words *EXCREMENT* and *FAECES* have developed in much the same way.

This meaning emerged at around the time that *shit* was falling out of use as Standard English and starting its twilight existence as a so-called vulgarism. *Crap* was presumably used originally as a euphemism, although it never seems to have gained full respectability, and indeed is now regarded as something of a vulgarism itself.

The popular story that the word *crap* is derived from the name of Thomas Crapper, a manufacturer of Victorian lavatory porcelain, is unfortunately not true. It seems to have been based upon an elaborate hoax.

CRUMPET

(*col.*) *An attractive woman.*

The word has been in use with this sense since the 1880s, but its origins are far from certain. One possibility is that it was originally used as a euphemism for '*buttered bun*', a much older term which was already regarded as vulgar by that time.

The term *buttered bun* referred to a woman who had had sexual intercourse with a number of men in quick succession. It has been in continuous use from the sixteenth century to the present day.

For other food terms applied to women see TART.

CUCKOLD

As a noun, a man whose wife is unfaithful to him; as a verb, to be unfaithful to one's husband or to commit adultery with another man's wife.

Thus, if Mr A has an affair with Mrs B then they are both cuckolding Mr B, and Mr B is a cuckold.

The term comes from the Old French word *cucault* which meant both 'cuckoo' and 'cuckold'. The connection seems to be that the European cuckoo occupies other birds' nests and leaves its young for others to rear.

Cuckoldry has always been a great English comic theme. It was a favourite of both Chaucer and Shakespeare, as it was in Restoration comedy, and continues to be in modern farce.

CULLION

(obs.) A testicle, also a person of little worth.

Derived from the French *couillon*, which shares the same dual meaning, the word has been in use for many centuries. Its original meaning was 'testicle', but as with so many terms associated with sex, it was subsequently adopted as a term of abuse.

In the following passage, from *The Pardoner's Tale* (C 948–55), Chaucer used the word in its original sense:

> . . . Thou wouldst make me kiss thine old breach
> And swear it were a relic of a saint
> Though it were with thy fundament depaint [stained]
> But, by the cross which Saint Helen found
> I would I had thy cullions in my hand
> Instead of relics or of saintuary [holy things]
> Let's cut them off, I will thee help them carry
> They should be enshrined in a hog's turd . . .

33

Shakespeare used the word in its other sense in *The Second Part of Henry VI* (I. iii. 38): 'Away, base cullions!'; and adapted it as an adjective in *King Lear* (II. ii. 33): 'You whoreson cullionly barbermonger'.

CUNNILINGUS

Oral stimulation of the female genitals.

The word's meaning is immediately apparent from its constituent Latin elements *cunnus*, female genitals, and *lingere*, to lick.

Alternative terms are *cannibalism*, *eating a kipper feast*, *muff diving*, *pearl diving*, *eating FUR PIE* or *hair pie* or *a furburger*, *tonguing*, *French kissing*, *licking out*, and *whistling in the dark*.

CUNNY

(col.) Female genitals.

A euphemism for *cunt*, the word is apparently derived from the word *cony* (or *coney*), once a common name for a rabbit. In fact until the last century *cony* was the Standard English term for the animal; only young ones were called *rabbits*. (Amongst other things this explains why the American island once infested by rabbits was named not *Rabbit Island* but *Coney Island*.)

Although the word *cony* is now generally pronounced 'cone-ee', its traditional pronunciation was 'cunny'. For centuries the two words *cony* and *cunny* existed side by side with the same pronunciation but distinct meanings. This created a degree of ambiguity and it is probably because of the consequent embarrassment that people started to pronounce the word *cony* as 'cone-ee'. Indeed the narrative to some versions of the Bible recommends that for solemn reading the 'cone-ee' pronunciation should be adopted.

The traditional pronunciation of *cony* is apparent in the mercenary sentiment '. . . No money, no coney', a rhyming pun from *The Virgin Martyr* (II. i.) by Massinger, 1622.

The mix-up between the words reflects an ancient similarity between the Latin words *cunnus*, meaning female genitals, and *cuniculus*, originally meaning 'rabbit' but later extended to burrows or passageways. This, along with the rabbit's well-known disposition for sexual incontinence, largely explains the association between *conies* and *cunnies*.

There is a further parallel with the word *PUSSY*, another euphemism for the female genitals. Although the name *Puss* is now generally associated with cats, in earlier times it was customarily applied to rabbits and hares.

Cunny-hunter and *cunny-warren* are obsolete terms for a whore-monger and a brothel respectively.

CUNT

(col.) The female genitals.

Possibly derived from the Anglo-Saxon *cynd*, the Middle English form of the word was *kunte*, the same form used in Dutch and other Low German languages. It is clearly related to the Icelandic *kunta*, and there can be little doubt that both are derived from a word which must have existed in a common Germanic language over two thousand years ago.

This ancient language was itself evolved as an offshoot of another, older, language known as Proto-Indo-European, which probably existed between four and six thousand years ago. Philologists believe that in this language the sound *ku* may have been used to mean much the same as the modern English *cunt*, and that indeed the word *cunt* is ultimately derived from it. This being so, we might reasonably expect to find similar derivatives in other Indo-European languages.

In fact there are a number of such languages which do have similar words: *kun* in Persian for example means rump or posterior, and the same word in Hittite meant tail. In Ancient Greek the word *konnos* also meant posterior. Another relation is the Latin *cunnus* (see CUNNY), and thence the Italian *conno* and French *CON*, all of which correspond in meaning to the English *cunt*.

Until the Middle Ages, parts of the body and bodily functions were accepted as commonplace facts of life, and the names for them were used as freely as any other word. Any part of the body which was unusually large or small, or unusually coloured, or otherwise

35

remarkable was likely to provide a convenient nickname or surname for its owner. So it is that we find recorded women's names such as *Gunoka Cuntles* (1219) and *Bele Wydecunthe* (1328), and men's names such as *Godwin Clawecuncte* (1066), *Simon Sitbithecunte* (1167), *John Fillecunt* (1246) and *Robert Clevecunt* (1302). In the City of London there was, in 1230, a street called *Gropecuntlane*.

Throughout the fourteenth century, and in certain areas for a long time afterwards, the word continued to be used without impropriety. Lanfranc, in his *Science of Chirurgie* (172, 12) written early in the fifteenth century, wrote: 'In women the neck of the bladder is short, & is made fast to the cunte'.

The authoritative *Survey of English Dialects* prepared in the 1950s and 60s, revealed that in rural areas the word was still being used as an ordinary everyday term, at least when applied to a cow's vulva. In mainstream English, however, the word has been avoided in writing and polite conversation since around the end of the fourteenth century. Chaucer, for example, did not use the word, although his substitution of the word *queynte* is obvious enough (see QUAINT). Shakespeare also avoided the word, though many of his puns show that it is to be understood (see CONSTABLE and COUNTRY).

Since the beginning of the eighteenth century the word has been held to be obscene, and it has been an offence to print it in full except in the reprinting of old classics. Eric Partridge notes a pythonesque line in *The Spanish Curate* (by John Fletcher, 1622): 'They write sunt with a C, which is abominable'.

The original edition of the *Oxford English Dictionary* avoided the word altogether, although later supplements have included it, following the example of the *Penguin English Dictionary* which first included it in 1965. Even now, the word is usually confined to private usage and is much less likely to be heard on the wireless or seen in newspapers than the word *fuck*.

In Cockney rhyming slang the word adopts many guises, for example *grumble and grunt*, *grasp and grunt*, *growl and grunt*, and *sharp and blunt*. See also BERK, CHARLIE, and JOEY.

Other ways of surreptitiously using the word without actually saying it include the dismissive phrase '*see you next Tuesday*' – supposedly representing the letters C-U-N-T, and *tenuc*, an example of back slang with the additional 'e' having been introduced to make it easier to pronounce.

CURSE, THE

(col.) A woman's menstrual period.

The reference is to the '*Curse Of Eve*' a biblical event reported in Genesis (3: 16). God, with his characteristic beneficence says to Eve 'I will greatly multiply thy sorrow and thy conception: in sorrow thou shalt bring forth children . . .'.

It is not at all obvious that this passage is intended to refer to menstruation; but the term is nevertheless well established. Elsewhere in the Bible the matter is dealt with with considerable delicacy: '. . . it ceased to be with Sarah after the manner of women' (Genesis 18: 11).

Most terms for menstruation make reference to its characteristic cycle of around four weeks. *Monthly period* clearly falls into this category, as does the word *menstruation* itself, *menses* being the Latin word for 'months'. The Anglo–Saxon term was *monathlican*, literally 'monthlies'. Incorporated in it is the word *mona*, meaning both 'moon' and 'month'.

D

DAISY CHAIN

(*col.*) *A chain of homosexual men, each engaged in anal intercourse with the one in front.*

Along with other expressions such as *chain gang* and *floral arrangement*, which employ similar imagery, this one has apparently been in use since the 1950s.

DAMN

As a noun, a curse; as a verb, to curse.

The word is adapted from the French *damner*, ultimately from the Latin *damnare* meaning to condemn.

Once an extremely strong word, it was widely avoided in conversation and could be printed only in a disguised form, for example as *D****. Bowdler, in his famous expurgated version of the works of Shakespeare (1818), found it necessary to amend the well-known line from *Macbeth* (v. i. 35) 'Out, damned spot!' to 'Out, crimson spot!'.

To disguise the word in speech it might become *darn* or *dang*, and similarly *damnation* may become *tarnation*. Such disguised oaths may still be heard, especially in the USA, despite the fact that *damn* itself is no longer strongly tabooed.

DILDO

An artificial penis.

Since the sixteenth century this word has been used in two ways. As well as a term for a penis substitute it was also used as a nonsense word to fill out songs (in much the same way as *hey-nonny-no*).

It is not at all clear which sense Shakespeare had in mind when in *The Winter's Tale* (IV. iv. 193–6) a servant says that Autolycus has

... The prettiest love-songs for maids; so without bawdry, which is strange; with such delicate burthens of dildos and fadings, 'jump her and thump her' ...

As usual, the best bet is to assume that he knew and meant both senses. Incidentally, no one now knows what is meant by *'fading'*, but, as the *Oxford English Dictionary* notes, *'with a fading'* was the refrain of a popular song of an indecent character.

The origin of the word *dildo* is also something of a mystery. Often where little or no early documentary evidence exists, useful clues can be gained by looking at corresponding terms in other European languages. In this case, however, there is no help from the expectedly numerous French terms: *bienfaiteur* means literally 'do-gooder', *consolateur* means roughly 'relaxer', *godemiché* 'I enjoy myself' and *jacquot* 'Polly'.

To Italians it could be a *fascinum* (see FASCINATE), *passatempo* literally 'pass time', or *diletto* literally 'darling' or 'beloved'. This latter is as close as we can get to a likely ancestor of our *dildo*.

DILL

(col.) The penis, also a foolish or incompetent person.

The word has a Standard English meaning of 'pickled cucumber', but the similarity in shape long ago suggested the secondary meaning of 'penis'. Like many other terms for the penis it was subsequently adopted as a general purpose insult.

Especially popular in Australia, the term mirrors the British WALLY.

Dear Me!

An exclamation.

Not quite as meaningless as it appears, this expression is apparently a disguised *OATH*. The most likely theory as to its origin is that it is a corruption of *Dio mi (salvi)!*, an Italian phrase which translates as 'God save me!'.

Dick

(col.) The penis.

This is one of a number of men's names which are applied to the penis. See *JOHN*.

The word *dick* was first recorded with this sense only in the late nineteenth century, a fact which is consistent with its supposed origin as rhyming slang. The problem is that no one is sure what the original rhyme was. Although *dick* rhymes perfectly with *prick*, it is just as likely to be a shortened form of *dickory dock*, which is well-known rhyming slang for *cock*.

Dike also Dyke

(col.) A lesbian.

Having apparently originated in the USA, this term has now gained wide international currency.

Its origin is something of a mystery, but in the absence of any convincing evidence the most likely theory is that it refers to the dyke into which a finger was inserted in the story of The Little Dutch Boy. Lesbianism is closely associated in the popular imagination with '*finger-fucking*'.

Dilberries

(col.) 'Small pieces of excrement adhering to the hairs near the fundament' (1811 Dictionary of the Vulgar Tongue).

The word is not as widely used as it once was, but it certainly survives. In parts of the USA it has been corrupted to *dingle berries*. (See also FARTLEBERRIES.)

DIRT

Excrement, also pornography.

In the Middle Ages the word was spelled *drit* but, as in a number of English words, over the centuries the *r* and *i* exchanged places. The form *drit* had been borrowed from the Vikings and Danes who used it specifically to mean excrement. The King James' Bible uses the word in this sense, as, for example, in Judges (3: 21–2) where God's messenger Ehud murders King Eglon:

> And Ehud put forth his left hand, and took the dagger from his right thigh, and thrust it into his belly: and the haft also went in after the blade; and the fat closed upon the blade, so that he could not draw the dagger out of his belly; and the dirt came out.

In modern usage the word reflects a close association between three quite distinct ideas: earth, excrement, and sex. These different meanings are exemplified by a *dirty face*, a *dirty nappy*, and a *dirty magazine*.

The connection between earth and excrement is reflected in the word *soil: night-soil* is excrement, and *to soil one's clothes* is to beray oneself. Again the connection may be seen in the use of the word *BOG*. A *bog* may equally be marshy ground or a lavatory. A similar connection is implicit in the word *slop*. What we now know euphemistically as *cow-slips* and *ox-slips* were originally '*cow-slops*' and '*ox-slops*'. The idea is much the same as that behind a more explicit German name for the cow-slip, *kuh scheisse* ('cow shit'), a reference to its favoured growing areas.

Other words combine the 'soil' and 'pornography' themes; for example, *muck*, *filth*, and *smut*. Even the word *obscene* is derived from a Latin word meaning mud or excrement.

In Johnson's Dictionary of 1755 the verb *to dirty* is comprehensively defined as 'to foul, to bemire, to make filthy, to bedaub, to soil; to pollute, to nasty'.

Dog

A male prostitute.

This euphemism is a reference to anal intercourse carried out 'doggy-fashion'.

It was the term favoured by the seventeenth century translators of the King James' Bible, a fact which helps to explain some passages which otherwise look a little odd. Deuteronomy (23: 18), for example, is actually a prohibition on temple prostitution:

> Thou shalt not bring the hire of a whore,
> or the price of a dog, into the house of
> the Lord thy God . . .

Doxy

A mistress, paramour, or prostitute.

The word's ultimate origin is uncertain but the *Oxford English Dictionary* suggests a connection with *dock* meaning 'buttocks' or 'tail'. As a verb *dock* originally meant to cut off a tail, a sense that we still preserve when we talk of *docking a horse's* or *dog's tail*. (The more general idea of cutting or reducing, as when we talk of *docking* someone's pay is a later extension of this idea.)

This theory is supported by the *1811 Dictionary of the Vulgar Tongue* which, under the headword *to dock*, gives the definition 'to lie with a woman'.

Although the word *doxy* is now regarded as archaic, it is still widely known. Whenever the words orthodoxy or heterodoxy are used they generally invite a pun along the lines of Bishop Warburton's in 1750: 'Orthodoxy, my Lord, is my doxy. Heterodoxy is another man's doxy'.

Drat It!

(col.) An exclamation.

Still in common use, this is an old disguised oath (see OATH). It is a corruption of the expression *God rot it!*

DUCK FUCKER

(*col.*) *A general term of abuse.*

According to the *1811 Dictionary of the Vulgar Tongue* the expression had a much more specific meaning. It was the informal title of 'The man who has the care of poultry on board a ship of war'.

DUCKING STOOL

A stool on to which scolds and nuisances were tied and sometimes ducked in water as a form of punishment.

This is a convenient euphemism for what was actually called a *cucking stool*.

A cucking stool was a close-stool, a primitive type of lavatory. The name means literally 'shitting stool' the word *cucking* being a variation of *cacking*, meaning to excrete (see CACK).

Johnson's Dictionary of 1755 has no entry for *ducking stool*, but under *cuckingstool* has 'An engine invented for the punishment of scolds and unquiet women, which, in ancient times, was called a tumbrel . . .'.

Throughout the country, sites of old cucking stools with names such as *Cuckstool Field* and *Cuckstool Meadow*, may still be found.

DUG

A female breast or nipple.

The word has many relatives amongst the Indo-European family of languages. All of them share a common progenitor, an ancient word which meant 'suckler' or 'milker'.

Once Standard English, it is now regarded as vulgar and has largely fallen into disuse.

In the following passage, Shakespeare uses the word without any hint of impropriety. The nurse in *Romeo and Juliet* (I. iii. 24–32), who had originally been Juliet's wet nurse, is wittering about how she had weaned her:

> ... And she was weaned, I shall never forget it,
> Of all the days of the year, upon that day;
> For I had then laid wormwood to my dug,
> Sitting in the sun under the dove-house wall;
> My lord and you were then at Mantua.
> Nay, I do bear a brain: – but as I said,
> When it did taste the wormwood on the nipple
> Of my dug and felt it bitter, pretty fool!
> To see it tetchy and fall out with the dug ...

By Samuel Johnson's time this neutrality was already gone. He defined the word as follows 'a pap; a nipple; a teat: spoken of beasts, or in malice or contempt of human beings ...'.

DUMB GLUTTON

(*col.*) *The female genitals.*

This is one of several expressions which humorously disguise an element of male apprehension about the nature of the vagina. Other such expressions include: *man trap*, *bottomless pit*, *biter*, *snapper*, and *vicious circle*.

DUNNY

(*col.*) *A lavatory, especially an outside one.*

Although it is now most popular in Australia, the word originated in seventeenth-century England. In early records it is found as *dunnaken*, *dunegan*, *dunnykin*, *dunna*, and *dunee*.

The etymology of the word is uncertain, but it is likely that the first part of it alludes to *dun*, the name of the characteristic brown colour which also appears in dung.

Other popular Australian names for the dunny include *diddy*, *toot*, and *brasco*.

DYKE

(*col.*) *See* DIKE.

E

ELEPHANT AND CASTLE

(*col.*) *The anus.*

Though it is rhyming slang for *arse hole*, the rhyme is non-existent for many speakers. In Cockney speech, however, the terms *arse hole* and *castle* rhyme perfectly, being pronounced something like '*arse-ow*' and '*carse-ow*' respectively.

EMERODS

Piles, haemorrhoids.

A variation of *haemorrhoids*, this is the form used in the King James' Bible. For example a divine threat from Deuteronomy (28:27) assures us that if we do not do what we are told then: 'The Lord will smite thee with the botch of Egypt, and with the emerods, and with the scab, and with the itch, whereof thou canst not be healed'.

Chapter 6 of the First Book of Samuel starts by relating that when the Philistines decided to return the ark of the covenant to the Israelites they were advised to include a 'trespass offering' to make amends. When asked what the trespass offering should be, the priests and diviners replied '. . . Five golden emerods, and five golden mice . . . wherefor ye shall make images of your emerods, and images of your mice . . .'. The significance of the emerods and mice is that these had been the vehicles by which God had previously punished the Philistines.

EXCREMENT

Faeces, shit.

Like the Latin *excrementum*, from which it is derived, this word originally meant 'that which is sifted out', in other words the unwanted part. Its original use in English was to denote dregs, leftovers and other refuse. In this respect it closely resembles the words *CRAP* and *FAECES*.

The following quotation from a Latin thesaurus of 1565 shows the word in the process of acquiring its new meaning: '*Excrementum*, the dregs or excrements of digestion made in the body; as phlegm, choler, melancholy, urine, sweat, snivell, spittel, milk, ordure'.

Excrement is also known, with varying degrees of seriousness, as *SHIT, TURDS, CACK*, *big-jobs, doings, poos, number twos, BUSINESS*, and *grunties*. See also PONY and RICHARD THE THIRD.

F

F.A., Sweet

(*col.*) '*Sweet fuck all*', *nothing*.

It seems that the expression *sweet F.A.* is not an abbreviation of *sweet fuck all*, but rather that *sweet fuck all* was invented to fit the older *sweet F.A.*

The original *F.A.* was *Frances Adams*, a little girl who was brutally murdered in 1867. This was around the time that tinned mutton was first bought by the Royal Navy, and the sailors humorously pretended that sweet Fanny Adams' dismembered body had found its way into their new tinned meat. They started to call the meat *sweet Fanny Adams*, and then, because they did not have a very high opinion of it, they started to refer to anything regarded as worthless by the same name. From meaning 'of no value' it was a short step for the expression to acquire the meaning 'nothing'.

Faeces

Excrement.

In Latin the word means sediment, dregs, or refuse, which is what it also meant in English until it was commandeered as a respectable alternative to *shit* and *turd*.

This development of meaning closely parallels that of the words *CRAP* and *EXCREMENT*.

FAG, FAG(G)OT

(col.) A male homosexual.

Principally American in usage, the word was first recorded in this sense, according to the *Supplement to the Oxford English Dictionary*, in 1914: 'All the faggots (sissies) will be dressed in drag at the ball tonight'.

The meaning is now well known in the UK, but the occasional Briton still causes a stir in the USA by using the word in one of its older senses. A few years ago a British diplomat surprised wireless listeners in the USA when he mentioned that another well-known personality had been his fag at Eton.

In conventional English a faggot is a bundle of sticks, but the word has long been used as a pejorative slang term for a woman. This probably explains the origin of the new American meaning, many names for women having been transferred to homosexual men. Other examples are *nancy, pansy, princess, jessie, lizzie, mary, nelly* and *QUEAN.*

FANNY

(col.) Female genitals (UK), or rump (USA).

The transatlantic difference in meaning renders the word broadly acceptable in the USA but less so in Britain. The difference causes a degree of misunderstanding.

In Britain, however, the word is also used as a perfectly respectable contraction of the name *Frances*. When the film *Fanny by Gaslight* was shown in America it had to have its title changed because of potential ambiguities about its content.

The current English meaning of 'female genitals' is certainly old, possibly predating John Cleland's famous book *Fanny Hill*, first published in 1749. In fact it is not at all certain whether the name *Fanny Hill* was a deliberate pun referring to the *MONS VENERIS* and depending upon an already current usage, or whether the word *fanny* originated from the name of Cleland's heroine.

Until fairly recently the American meaning was also current in England. In Noel Coward's *Private Lives* (1930), for example, he included the line 'You'd fallen on your fanny a few moments before'.

FART

(*col.*) *As a noun, gas expelled through the anus; as a verb, to expel gas through the anus.*

Since time immemorial the word had been Standard English, but in the last couple of centuries it has come to be regarded as improper.

In origin it is almost certainly echoic, the spelling being as near as we can get with conventional English to a sort of *pht* sound.

The following song was first recorded in 1250 by a Monk at Reading Abbey:

> Summer is icumen in
> Lhude sing cuckoo!
> Ewe bleateth after lamb
> Loweth after calve cu [cow lows after calf]
> Bullock starteth, bucke farteth,
> Merry sing, cuckoo!

Even in Chaucer's time there were those who were unduly sensitive about farting. In *The Miller's Tale* for example Absolon is described as 'somedeel squaymous of fartyng' (somewhat squeemish about farting).

In 1610, however, Ben Jonson had no qualms about starting his play *The Alchemist* with the memorable line 'I fart at thee . . .'; and in 1722 there appeared a pamphlet entitled *The Benefit of Farting Explain'd*, purportedly written in Spanish by *Don Fart in Hando* and translated into English by one *Obadiah Fizle*.

Quoting from Swift, Samuel Johnson in his 1755 Dictionary gives the following example of the word's use:

> As when we a gun discharge,
> Although the bore be ne'er so large,
> Before the flame from muzzle burst,
> Just at the breech it flashes first;
> So from my lord his passion broke,
> He farted first, and then he spoke.

The *1811 Dictionary of the Vulgar Tongue* notes the following usages under the headword fart: 'He has let a brewer's fart, grains and all; said of one who was bewrayed his breeches' and 'I dare not trust my arse with a fart: said by a person troubled with a looseness'.

In the same work *catch fart* and *fart catcher* are explained as meaning 'valet' or 'footman'. They were so called because they walked immediately behind their master or mistress. More recently however, the term *fart catcher* has been applied to male homosexuals.

Dating from the middle of the last century, the expression 'like a fart in a colander' is still in common use to indicate restlessness or any flustered aimless activity. So too, in some dialects the traditional name *mare's fart* is still used for the plant otherwise known as *fleabane*.

Although the Victorians have a largely deserved reputation for prudery, the music halls maintained a proud tradition for earthy humour. For years the highest paid performer in Europe was a Frenchman, one Joseph Pujol (1857–1945), who entertained his audiences with virtuoso performances of farting. Outshining Sarah Bernhardt, he was secretly given an OBE by the Prince of Wales, much to the annoyance of Queen Victoria. Using Debussy's 'Clare de lune' for accompaniment, he cut a record which proved so popular that Debussy's royalty income doubled when it was released.

The art was far from original, however. As St Augustine recorded in *The City of God* (14, 24) 'There are those that can break wind backwards so artfully you would think they sang'. He wrote this (in Latin) in AD 430.

Pujol's stage name was *Le pétomaine*, adapted from the French *un pet* meaning a fart. This word appears in a number of terms familiar on this side of the Channel. For example to be *hoist by one's own petard* is to be blown up by one's own 'farting-machine', an ancient engine of war.

In French the expression *péter plus haut que son cul*, literally to 'fart higher than one's arse' means to think too highly of oneself. *Péter le feu*, literally to 'fart fire' means to be full of energy; and the term *un péte-sec*, literally 'a clean, dry farter' is applied to any martinet.

In the sixteenth century habitual chatterers and babblers were known, rather picturesquely, as *clatterfarts*.

FARTLEBERRIES

(col.) Excrement adhering to the hair around the anus.

This term dates at least from the seventeenth century.

Alternative names include *BUMTAGS*, *CLINKERS*, *DIL-BERRIES*, and *winnets*.

FASCINATE

To spellbind, or hold bewitched.

Although this word is not itself taboo, the full details of its etymology are carefully avoided in many dictionaries.

Both the word and its association with magic can be traced back to the Latin *fascinum*, which denoted not only a magical spirit, but also a magical image to ward off evil spirits. In practice, the most potent image was believed to be a phallus, so the word was also used for a penis. To this day an Italian word for a dildo is *fascinum*.

In Italy, and many other Roman Catholic countries, sexual gestures and images are still used to ward off the evil eye, or to invite good luck (see FIG and TESTICLE).

FEAGUE

To insert objects into a horse's rectum to make it hold up its tail.

As the *1811 Dictionary of the Vulgar Tongue* explains: 'To feague a horse; to put ginger up a horse's fundament, and formerly, as it is said, a live eel, to make him lively and carry his tail well . . .'.

The word is not now widely used, presumably because the practice itself has largely fallen into disuse. On the other hand, we still use the phrase '*to ginger up*', and its etymology is apparently much the same.

FEEL

(*col.*) *To touch in sexually sensitive areas, to grope.*

This sense has run parallel to the more innocent conventional one for centuries. Here, for example, near the beginning of Shakespeare's *Romeo and Juliet*, are a series of double entendres:

SAMPSON. . . . the heads of the maids, or their maidenheads; take it in what sense thou will.

GREGORY. They must take it in the sense that feel it.

SAMPSON. Me they shall feel while I am able to stand: and 'tis known I am a pretty piece of flesh.

In the late seventeenth century a popular name for the female genitals was 'old hat', a pun which depended on the observation that they were 'both frequently felt'. Later, emancipated women made puns along the lines of 'happiness is a fellow feeling', and more recently such subtleties as 'I'm not feeling myself tonight' have provided titles for books and films.

FELLATIO

The act of sucking or licking a penis.

This word is first recorded in English only in 1887. It is clearly derived from the Latin *fellare*, to suck.

In keeping with this Latin origin, a man who fellates is known as a *fellator*, but a woman who does so is a *fellatrix*.

FEM

(*col.*) *A passive homosexual.*

The term may be applied both to men and women, but more usually to men. In Australia it is generally applied only to men.

It is based upon the French word for a woman, *femme*, and indeed, in English, this spelling is sometimes used for passive lesbians, in preference to *fem*.

FIFE AND DRUM

(*col.*) *Arse.*

This is another example of Cockney rhyming slang, the rhyme, of course, being with *bum*.

FIG

(*col.*) *A representation of the female genitals.*

As D. H. Lawrence noted in *Women in Love* figs have been identified with the female genitals since ancient times. The Greek word for a fig, for example, was used as a euphemism for the female pudendum. The French word for a fig, *figue*, is also used in this way, and the Italian counterpart of the English word *cunt* is *figa*, a close relative of *fico*, the Italian word for a fig.

It is significant that fruit of 'the tree of knowledge of good and evil' which Eve gave to Adam was not as is usually assumed an apple but, according to rabinical scholars, probably a fig (Genesis is not specific about the matter). In the story Adam and Eve certainly used fig leaves to cover their genitals.

In English the word *fig* is also applied to an insulting gesture made with the hand: the fist is closed and the thumb pushed through the index and middle fingers. It is intended to represent the female genitals. Originally it was used as a magical charm to ward off evil, the genitals, or images of them, being believed to carry supernatural power. Having survived from antiquity this gesture is now much less common in Britain than it once was, though it still flourishes in southern Europe both as a magical charm and an insult. To make the gesture in France is to *faire la figue*.

For centuries the word *fig* has been used as a synonym for *fuck*; but it is more likely that Shakespeare had the insulting gesture in mind in *The Second Part of Henry IV* (v. iii. 117–18) where Pistol says: 'When Pistol lies, do this; and fig me, like the bragging Spaniard'.

Jacobean writers often employed the Italian word *fico* as an expletive. Johnson's Dictionary mentions it but explains it as meaning 'An act of contempt done with the fingers, expressing a fig for you'

– the gesture described above. Our modern expressions about '*not giving a fig*' and '*not caring a fig*' are also references to this gesture.

The word *sychophant* is derived from an ancient Greek term which was used in much the same way as we use *sychophant*. The Greek word, however, had originally meant 'fig-displayer' but there is no very satisfactory explanation for its semantic development. The story given in many dictionaries – that it originally denoted an informer against exporters of contraband figs – is pure fantasy. In all probability the 'fig' referred to was a vulva, or a representation of a vulva.

FILTH

Dirt (in the metaphorical sense as well as the literal).

The adjective *filthy* has had a parallel metaphorical sense of 'impure' or 'obscene' for centuries. This sense is clearly apparent in *The First Part of Henry IV* (II. ii. 48) where Falstaff mentions ballads '. . . sung to filthy tunes'. See also DIRT.

In the sixteenth and seventeenth centuries prostitutes were referred to as *filth*, but since then the epithet has been inexplicably transferred to policemen.

FIRK, or FERK

(col.) Fuck.

Originally the word meant to beat or strike, and this appears to be the meaning intended in Shakespeare's *Henry V* (IV. iv. 26–9). Pistol is talking to a French soldier, using a boy to translate:

BOY. He says his name is Master Fer.
PISTOL. Master Fer! I'll fer him, and firk him and ferret him.
BOY. I do not know the French for fer, and ferret, and firk.

The similarity between *firk* and *fuck*, and the fact that they were both originally associated with violence, suggests that they may be related; indeed they may be mere variants of the same word. Certainly *firk* has been used for centuries as a synonym for *fuck*. Cotgave, in a 1611 glossary, defined *firkerie* as '. . . an odd pranke, or jerke, in whoorisme'.

What we now refer to as foreplay was in earlier centuries known as *FIRKYTOODLING*.

FIRKYTOODLING
See FIRK.

FLASH

(*col.*) *To show, especially something which ought not to be seen.*

In the eighteen hundreds there were a large number of expressions in common usage employing this word. A *flash tail*, for example, was a harlot, and a woman who *flashed the upright grin* was one who exposed her genitals.

A man who exposed his genitals was said to *flash the meat*, hence the modern term *flasher*.

Another expression preserved from this time is *flash the hash*, meaning to vomit.

FLUTE

(*col.*) *The penis.*

Popular variations in the eighteenth century included *silent flute*, *living flute*, and *one holed flute*.

In this century Barry Humphries has repopularized many expressions of this type.

FLYING PASTY

(*col.*) *Excrement wrapped in paper and thrown over a neighbour's wall.*

This expression, first recorded around 1790, has largely fallen into disuse along with the particular form of antisocial behaviour associated with it.

FORNICATION

Illicit sexual activity.

Properly the term refers specifically to sexual intercourse between two unmarried people. In practice, however, it is applied to any adulterous or unsanctioned sexual activity.

The word's origin can easily be traced back to the Latin *fornix*, meaning 'brothel'. This meaning, however, was secondary, the primary one being 'arch' or 'vault'. The connection is a direct result of the Roman's custom of locating their brothels in vaults with arched roofs.

As in Latin, so in English. *Fornication* bears a corresponding dual meaning, referring as it does in architectural jargon to an arch or vault.

FOUR LETTER WORDS

Words regarded as obscene.

Such words are generally associated with sex or excretion. They are mostly Anglo-Saxon in origin and were once everyday standard terms. Over the last few hundred years they have come to be regarded as somehow improper and have been replaced by a succession of euphemisms and classical genteelisms.

Typical examples are *ARSE*, *BALL(S)*, *CACK*, *COCK*, *COME*, *CUNT*, *FART*, *FRIG*, *FUCK*, *PISS*, *PRAT*, *QUIM*, *SHAG*, *SHIT*, *TURD*, *TWAT*, and *WANK*.

In polite circles the ubiquitous French word *merde* ('shit') is known as *les cinq lettres*.

FRECKLE

(col.) The anus.

A popular term in Australia, it is likely to be misunderstood in the UK where it is used only to denote the familiar small brown skin markings.

Other Australianisms for this part of the anatomy which are not yet well known in the UK include *quoit* and *blurter*.

FRENCH SICKNESS (also FRENCH GOUT)

Venereal disease.

As in more recent times with AIDS, it has long been customary for nations to blame each other for the introduction of sexually transmitted diseases. For example the Germans called VD the *Spanish scabies*, the Spanish know it as the *French disease*, and the French named it the *Neapolitan* or *Italian malady*.

There has always been an element of mutual animosity in the framing of French and English terms. In the sixteenth century, for example, a creditor was called in French *un Anglais*; and it is well known that what we call *French leave* is to the French *filer à l'anglaise*. Again, our *French letter* is, on the other side of the Channel, *une capote anglaise*. The *1811 Dictionary of the Vulgar Tongue* explains the phrase 'He suffered a blow over the snout with a French faggot-stick' as 'he lost his nose by the pox'.

Our sexual xenophobia is, if anything, slightly less severe than that of the French. *French kissing* for example is relatively mild, even when applied to oral sex. A *French print* is an erotic picture, and *French lessons* generally involve sexual activities of various kinds. To the French, however, homosexuality and sometimes flagellation is *le vice anglais* (the English vice), and to menstruate is to *avoir les anglaises* (to have the Englishes).

FRIG

(col.) To masturbate.

Although this meaning was first recorded in the late sixteenth century, the word itself is at least a hundred years older. Its original meaning was to rub.

It is derived from the Latin *fricare*, also meaning to rub (from which, incidentally, we have the word *friction*).

FUCK

(*col.*) *As a noun, sexual intercourse; as a verb, to copulate.*

Unlike most old words associated with sex, this one seems always to have been regarded as improper. Its origin is uncertain and has been the subject of much speculation.

The word has been around since at least the sixteenth century, and it may well be much older, although there is no written record of it. Chaucer uses synonyms such as *SWIVE* and *dighte*, both without any suggestion of impropriety.

It is likely that *fuck* is indirectly related to the Latin verb *pungere*, to the French *foutre*, and to the German *ficken*. All of these words have a principal meaning of 'to beat' or 'to strike', and a secondary one of 'to copulate'. There are, in fact, a surprisingly large number of words, both in English and in other languages, which share this double meaning combining violence and sex, see BONK.

Shakespeare never used the word *fuck* itself; nevertheless, there is no doubt that he knew it, and contrived deliberate puns on it. In *The Merry Wives of Windsor* (IV. i. 42–7) he plays on the word *focative*, and elsewhere uses *FIRK* and *foot* (see the quotation given at CON).

Although he was apparently unwilling to use the word explicitly, he was less worried by its French counterpart. In *The Second Part of Henry IV* (v. iii. 98) Pistol says 'A foutre for the world and worldlings base'; and again (at line 114) he says 'A foutre for thine office', in much the same way as we might talk about '*giving a fuck*'.

The Earl of Rochester (1647–80) was rather less inhibited than Shakespeare. His poems contained such lines as:

> . . . much wine had past with grave discourse
> of who fucks who, and who does worse . . .[4]

but, with a few such notable exceptions, the trend up until the last few decades has increasingly been to avoid the word in print.

A modern method of using the word without actually saying it is to employ phrases such as '*if you see Kate*', supposedly representing the letters F-U-C-K. A favourite of children, its use often goes unnoticed by adults.

[4] Quoted by Robert Burchfield in *Fair of Speech* (see Bibliography) from *Rochester's Poems on Several Occasions*, ed. James Thorpe (1950).

In the East End of London there are a number of possibilities for slang rhymes. A fuck can be a *cattle truck*, *trolley and truck*, *Friar Tuck*, or *Russian duck*. To fuck is *to push in the truck* and to get fucked is to be *cattle trucked*, or more simply to be *cattled*. So, too, the expletive *fuck it!* becomes *Mrs Duckett!* On the west coast of the USA where there is also a tradition of rhyming slang *lame duck* is used in preference to *Russian duck*, and the expression *goose and duck* has been shortened to *GOOSE*.

Because of the social taboos about the word *fuck* it is not unknown for considerable enjoyment to be generated by tricking someone into saying the word in public. For this reason the following lines, articulated at speed for the best effect, are popular in pubs and bars almost everywhere:

> I'm not the pheasant plucker,
> I'm the pheasant plucker's mate,
> And I'm only plucking pheasants
> 'cause the pheasant plucker's late.

As well as *foutre* the French also use *baiser* as a synonym for *fuck*. This provides extensive scope for embarrassment among foreigners learning the language: since *le baiser* means 'the kiss' students often assume that *baiser* means not 'to fuck' but 'to kiss', as indeed it once did. The French replacement for 'to kiss' is *embrasser*.

FUCKWIT

(*col.*) *A person of limited intellectual capacity.*

Originally Australian, this expression has proved sufficiently graphic to have gained considerable currency around the world.

FUR PIE

(*col.*) *The female genitals.*

Fur has been used as a slang term for pubic hair since at least the eighteenth century.

The word *furbelow*, properly denoting a plaited border, provides a similar, more obvious, pun.

To *eat fur pie* or *a furburger* is to practice *CUNNILINGUS*.

G

GADZOOKS!

An archaic exclamation.

A favourite of boys' comic books, this is an ancient disguised oath (see OATH).

It is a corruption of the expression *God's hooks*, a reference to the hooks or nails by which Jesus was pinned to the cross.

In earlier times the word *hook* was understood to refer to a bent nail, so *Gadzooks!* was probably thought marginally less silly than *S'nails!* the usual short form of *God's nails!*

GANG BANG

(col.) Group sex, or gang rape.

This term appears to have originated in the US navy around the early 1950s.

Alternative names are *gang shag* (US), *gang splash* (Australia), and *pig-party* (UK).

GASH

(col.) The vagina.

The term has been in continuous use since the eighteenth century. It is one of a group of words for the vagina and vaginal labia which draw on the imagery of cut flesh. Others are *wound*, *cat with its throat cut*, and *beef curtains*.

In the eighteenth century the expression '*to be in a woman's beef*' meant to have sexual intercourse with her. '*To be in a man's beef*', however, was to wound him with a sword.

Gay

(*col.*) *Homosexual.*

Although this sense of the word was recorded early in the century, it was not until the 1960s that its popularity increased to the extent that this meaning started to displace the conventional one.

In fact *gay* has had a secondary sexual meaning for centuries. To *be gay* was to be wanton or promiscuous. A *gay house* was a brothel, a *gay bit* a prostitute, and a *gaying instrument* a penis. *Leading a gay life* was, and still is, a euphemism for living by prostitution, as also was the expression *to go gay*.

Shakespeare clearly knew this meaning. In *Othello* (II. i. 151), Iago says that his ideal woman '. . . Never lacked gold, and yet went never gay'.

Gee!

(*col.*) *An exclamation.*

Essentially a shortened form of the name *Jesus*, this disguised oath continues to be popular in the USA. It is essentially the same as *JEEZE!* and *GEE-WHIZZ!*

Gee-Whizz!

(*col.*) *A children's exclamation.*

Popular in the USA, this is another corruption of *Jesus*. It is essentially the same as *GEE!* and *JEEZE!*

Gert Stonkers

(*col.*) *Large breasts.*

Gert is an ancient variation of the word *great*, though the etymology of *stonkers* is more doubtful.

The expression reputedly originated in rural dialect, but is now more widely used, presumably because of its onomatopoeic vividness. See also NORMA SNOCKERS.

GET

(*col.*) *Bastard.*

The word originally denoted any child, not necessarily an illegitimate one. Children were so described because, like any offspring, they are '*begotten*'. The earliest use recorded by the *Oxford English Dictionary* is dated 1320 'Myne owne gete ys fro me take' (My own get is from me taken).

In Northern usage the word has long had disparaging connotations. Like the word *brat* it has become increasingly pejorative and for centuries has been synonymous with *bastard*. In some dialects, however, the word is still applied to animals with its original neutral meaning.

GOB

(*col.*) *As a noun, either the mouth or a lump of phlegm; as a verb, to spit.*

While not being regarded as altogether improper, this word occupies a twilight world of not-quite-nice words avoided by the sensitive.

The word has for centuries been Standard English for any slimy clot, but especially one of phlegm or spittle. It is still widely used in dialect and also in certain industries, such as glass making.

As a term for the mouth we still freely accept it in the compound *gobstopper*, but otherwise it is often avoided. For example, we now prefer to speak of the *gift of the gab* rather than the *gift of the gob* as we once did.

GOD!

An exclamation.

Although the taboo is now less rigidly enforced, many people still regard it as somehow improper to talk of God without good cause. In particular, it has long been thought wrong to call upon God to witness trivial matters.

The underlying concern is that it is presumptuous, and therefore dangerous and sinful, to call upon a powerful deity. One may incur supernatural displeasure by disturbing the divine repose. It is also for this reason that the Devil should not be mentioned by name: 'Talk of the Devil and he will appear'. *Deuce* and *dickens* are both ancient, but still popular, evasions of the name of the Devil.

Over the centuries many oaths calling upon God have degenerated into exclamations. These are strictly *SWEAR-WORDS*, but are in no sense obscene.

To disguise the name of God, but retain the curious pleasure of making an exclamation, it was, and still is, a common practice to disguise the awful word. Hence *gad!*, *begad!* (By God!), *egad!*, *goodness!*, *GOLLY!*, *GOSH!*, and *GUM!*

Some of the oaths of this type have fallen out of use, although they are still familiar through historical writings and plays. Examples are *God's teeth!*, *'sblood!* (God's blood), *'od's bodkins!* (God's dear body), and *'od's fish!* (originally God's flesh). For contemporary examples see the entry at OATH.

GOLLY!

(*col.*) *An exclamation.*

Surprising as it may seem, this is a corruption of, and euphemism for, *GOD!*

GONORRHOEA

A venereal disease.

In previous centuries the characteristic discharge associated with this disease was thought to be semen. Indeed, this belief explains the name *gonorrhoea*: it is composed of Greek elements meaning 'semen-flow'.

GOOLIES

(*col.*) *The testicles.*

The word is relatively recent in origin, its earliest appearance in print being in 1937, although it was probably used in speech well before then.

It was apparently introduced from India, probably through the British army. In Hindustani the word *goli* is used to denote a round object such as a bullet, pebble, or ball; and it is very likely that this, or a similar term from a related Indian language, gave rise to our word.

Significantly, in Australia the word *gooly* was originally recorded as a slang term for a stone or pebble: a fact which supports the connection with *goli*. Its first appearance coincided with the Second World War, which is also consistent with its having been spread by the armed forces.

GOOSE

(*col.*) *To copulate with, or more generally to touch in a sexually sensitive area.*

The earliest meaning was 'to copulate with', which is not surprising given the origin of the term. To goose is really to *goose and duck*, rhyming slang for *FUCK*.

GOR BLIMEY!

(*col.*) *An exclamation.*

Still popular, this is an old disguised oath (see OATH).

It is a corruption of the expression *God blind me!*, as in expressions such as 'may God blind me (if I lie)'.

GOSH!

(*col.*) *An exclamation.*

Like *GOLLY*, this is a corruption of and euphemism for *GOD!* In the sixteenth century it took the form *gosse!*

GRIND

(*col.*) *To copulate.*

This is one of the many words for copulation that have survived for centuries. This one dates from the sixteenth century. At that time it was generally used in the expression *to do a grind*.

GUM!

(*col.*) *An exclamation.*

The original nineteenth-century form was *by gom!*, a disguised form of *by God!*

GUTS

Intestines, also courage.

Since ancient times the bowels were thought to be the seat of physical courage, an idea which is probably associated with the lack of bowel control experienced in times of acute fear (see BOTTLE). This link is also reflected in the word *pluck*. Like guts it can be used for both innards and courage.

The word *guts* was Standard English for centuries, being derived from the Anglo-Saxon *guttas*, which had exactly the same meaning. Since the beginning of the last century it has become offensive to some people. The country is now fairly evenly divided between those who talk of *tummies* and find words like *guts* and *belly* offensive, and those who talk of *guts* and *bellies*, and find words like *tummy* offensive.

The *1811 Dictionary of the Vulgar Tongue* explains the phrase 'My great guts are ready to eat my little ones' as one signifying great hunger. 'A plaister of warm guts' is defined as 'one warm belly clapped to another; a recipe frequently prescribed for different disorders'.

H

HAG

An ugly woman.

In earlier centuries the word denoted a witch, and was as likely to be applied to an attractive one as to any other. The association of witchcraft and ugly old women in the popular mind has given rise to the word's current meaning.

To be *hag-ridden* was literally to be ridden by a witch or other supernatural creature. At night, witches were thought to use people or animals to carry them to their sabbats. (The idea of using a broomstick was very much less common. Witches' broomsticks were principally phallic objects and were often explicitly carved as such.)

Hag riding provided a convenient explanation for a number of phenomena such as nightmares, irrational night terrors, and physical exhaustion upon waking up.

In Shakespeare's *Romeo and Juliet* (I. iv. 89–96) Mercutio talks at some length about a hag, Queen Mab:

> . . . This is that very Mab
> That plats the mains of horses in the night;
> And bakes the elf-locks in foul sluttish hairs,
> Which once untangled much misfortune bodes;
> This is the hag, when maids lie on their backs,
> That presses them and learns them first to bear,
> Making them women of good carriage;
> This is she—.

Upon being challenged by Romeo for talking about nothing, Mercutio replies 'True I talk of dreams . . .'.

The original meaning of the word *nightmare* is similar. A nightmare was a malicious spirit which oppressed its victims as they slept by sitting or lying on them. This type of mare is nothing to do with horses. It is the sort referred to in the expression *mare's nest*. To *uncover a mare's nest* is to expose a nest of evil spirits.

In the Middle Ages erotic dreams and spontaneous nocturnal emissions could conveniently be blamed on sexually inspired phantom witches and mares. Indeed, the phenomenon was so well established that there are names for specific types of phantom believed to sexually excite innocent sleepers. A phantom who takes a female form to excite men is a *succubus*, one who adopts a male form to excite women is an *incubus*.

HARLOT

A prostitute.

In previous centuries the word was used as a general term of opprobrium, and could be applied equally to men and women. In fact in its earliest recorded use in the thirteenth century it was applied specifically to men.

The original form of the word in Old French was *harlot* or *arlot*. It first meant 'vagabond', 'beggar', or 'rogue', but later developed the meaning of 'one of loose morals', and thus 'fornicator'. From there it is only a short step to its modern meaning.

The Old French form of the word is preserved in England in the surname *Arlot*.

HIDE THE SAUSAGE

(col.) To copulate.

This is a popular Australian expression which employs an ancient and obvious metaphor for the penis.

The phrase belongs to a long line of 'humorous' phrases for sexual intercourse. Another recent Australian one is *exercise the ferret* (or *armadillo*), but from as far back as the eighteenth century we have expressions such as *dance a blanket hornpipe*, *make feet for children's stockings*, indulge in *basket* (*i.e. bastard*) *making*, have a *knee trembler*, and enjoy a *plaster of warm guts*.

HOLE

(*col.*) *The vagina, also the anus.*

This is one of many words for the vagina which make reference to it simply as an orifice (see CRACK). This is also true when it is used as a term for the anus.

Chaucer uses the word apparently without impropriety in *The Miller's Tale* where, speaking of Alison, he says 'At the window out she put her hole' (see a fuller quotation under ARSE). It is however difficult to tell exactly which of her two possible 'holes' he is referring to.

Shakespeare is more circumspect in his use of the word, but the implication is clear enough. In *Romeo and Juliet* (II. iv. 93–103) Mercutio is complaining about Romeo's infatuation; in this passage the word *natural* means 'fool', and *bauble* (literally a child's toy) means 'penis', as also does *tale*, a pun on *TAIL*:

MERCUTIO. ... this drivelling love is like a great natural, that runs lolling up and down to hide his bauble in a hole.
BENVOLIO. Stop there, stop there.
MERCUTIO. Thou desirest me to stop in my tale against the hair.
BENVOLIO. Thou would'st else have made thy tale large.
MERCUTIO. O! Thou art deceived; I would have made it short; for I was come to the whole depth of my tale, and meant to occupy the argument no longer.

In the following passage, taken from the erotic Song of Songs in the King James' Bible, Bilqis, Queen of Sheba, is talking about her lover, King Solomon, who apparently suffered from premature ejaculation:

My beloved put his hand by the hole *of the door*,[5]
And my bowels were moved for him.
I rose up to open to my beloved;
And my hands dropped with myrrh,
And my fingers with sweet smelling myrrh,
Upon the handles of the lock
I opened to my beloved;
But my beloved had withdrawn himself ...
(Song of Solomon 5: 4–6)

[5] *of the door* these words are italicized in the Authorized Version because they were inserted by the translators. They do not exist in the original Hebrew text.

The frankness of the sexual imagery in this book of the Bible has caused great problems to Christian theologians throughout the centuries. It is only in the last few decades that they have stopped pretending that it is merely an allegory about the relationship between Christ and his Church.

HOMOSEXUAL

A man or woman sexually attracted to members of his or her own sex.

It is sometimes assumed that, since *homo* in Latin means 'man', this word is applicable only to men. This assumption, however, is mistaken: the first element of *homosexual* is derived not from the Latin *homo* but from the Greek *homos* meaning 'same'.

The English language has generated many terms for male homosexuals. Among the best known are *homo, queer, fairy, fruit, ponce*, and *shirt lifter*. See also *POOF, QUEAN, FAG* and *BUM-JUMPER*. A female homosexual might be called a *LESBIAN, sappist,* or *DIKE*. Both male and female homosexuals may be described as a *GAY* or a *FEM*.

HOOKER

(col.) A prostitute.

The word is chiefly used in the USA.

It was first recorded with this meaning in the USA in 1845. Its origin is uncertain but it is likely to have been derived from the Dutch *hoeker* meaning 'hukster'.

HORN

(col.) The erect penis.

The word has been in use with this sense for centuries. It is clearly a metaphor, likening the shape of an animal horn to that of a penis.

Because of this association various kinds of horn have traditionally been regarded as aphrodisiacs. In the East, rhinoceros horns are still in demand for this purpose. In the West, narwhal tusks were once favoured, often being passed off as unicorns' horns.

In Shakespeare's *The Taming of the Shrew* (IV. i. 25–7) Grumio uses the term fairly explicitly: 'Am I but three inches? Why, thy horn is a foot; and so long am I at least'.

To *get the horn*, or *suffer horn colic*, is to experience an erection, and to *cure the horn* is to have sexual intercourse.

The fungus known as *stinkhorn* is well known for its two chief characteristics. One is its disgusting smell and the other its remarkable similarity in appearance to an erect penis. Its Latin name also reflects this similarity: *phallus impudicus*, meaning 'shameless penis'.

From the word *horn* we have developed the adjective *horny* meaning sexually excited. Originally it was applied only to men, but is now equally applicable to men and women.

Historically *horn* has had a second sexual association. Cuckolds have traditionally worn horns to signify their wives' infidelity, hence to *wear the horns* is to suffer cuckoldry, and to be *horn mad* is to be passionately angry at having been cuckolded.

Horny

(col.) Sexually excited. See HORN.

Hot

(col.) Sexually excited.

This imagery has occurred to many cultures throughout history. Shakespeare sums up the position in *Troilus and Cressida* (III. i. 126–9):

> He eats nothing but doves, love; and that breeds hot love, and hot love begets hot thoughts, and hot thoughts beget hot deeds, and hot deeds is love.

To be *hot-arsed* is to be lascivious, and prostitutes are sometimes known as *hot beef*, *hot mutton*, or *hot meat*. *Hot pants* are sexy shorts, and to have *the hots* for someone is to be sexually attracted to them. Semen is occasionally called *hot milk* and sexual intercourse a *hot roll with cream*.

By contrast, those who never get hot in this sense are said to be *frigid*.

HUFFLE

(*col.*) *See* BAGPIPE.

HUMP

(*col.*) *To copulate.*

This is one of numerous English words for sexual intercourse which over the centuries periodically come into and go out of fashion. In the *1785 Dictionary of the Vulgar Tongue* it was described as 'once a fashionable word for copulation'.

HUSSY

A forward or shameless woman.

The word is actually a corruption of *housewife*, and the change of meaning has presumably come about because of too much gossip about brazen young housewives.

Hussif is an intermediate form of the word which represents an old pronunciation of *housewife*. It survives in dialect, and also as the name of a sewing kit.

I

IT

(col.) Any taboo subject.

This is a general purpose euphemism, popular for any sensitive subject from lavatories to sex.

In the expression *to have it*, the 'it' is sexual intercourse. Shakespeare uses the phrase in his 'Sonnets to Sundry Notes of Music' (IV, [23–24]):

> Had women been so strong as men,
> In faith, you had not had it then.

The catch phrase *it's naughty but nice* dates from the early part of this century, when its sexual innuendo was popular in music halls; but *it* also has a more general meaning of sexual attraction. The early film star Clara Bow, for example, was popularly known as the *it girl*.

ITCH

(col.) The sexual urge.

This meaning dates from the sixteenth century at least, especially in the expression *to have an itch in the belly*.

Since scratching generally assuages itching this word has also acquired a secondary sexual meaning of 'to satisfy sexually'. In *The Tempest* (II. ii. 54–5) Shakespeare has Stephano sing of Kate '. . . Yet a tailor [i.e. virtually anyone] might scratch where'er she did itch . . .'.

To *play itch buttocks* is to have sexual intercourse, and to experience a *seven-year itch* is to feel the need for additional sexual relationships, traditionally required after seven years of marriage.

J

JACK-OFF

(*col.*) *See* JERK.

JAKES

A lavatory.

Now rarely used, this word was for centuries a popular term accepted as Standard English.

In *King Lear* (II. ii. 74–6) Shakespeare uses it when he makes Kent propose to: '. . . tread this unbolted villain into mortar, and daub the walls of a jakes with him . . .'.

Many families which bear the surname *Jacques* would have originally spelled their name *Jakes*, but at some stage changed it because of its lavatorial associations. After all, it would not be much fun nowadays to have a name like 'Toilet'.

The plant commonly known as *jack-by-the-hedge*, a member of the cabbage family often found near hedgerows, is really a '*jakes-by-the-hedge*'. It was so called because of its unmistakable lavatorial smell.

For other lavatorial terms see LAVATORY.

JEEPERS CREEPERS!

(*col.*) *An exclamation.*

The expression is deliberately meaningless, being a disguised oath. It is a corruption of *Jesus Christ!* (see OATH).

JEEZE!

(*col.*) *An exclamation.*

Like *GEE!*, this is a disguised form of the name *Jesus*. See OATH.

The word has a long history, and was certainly popular in the Middle Ages. Shakespeare knew it, but spelled it *Gis*. Ophelia in *Hamlet* (IV. iv. 56–61) exclaims:

> By Gis and by Saint Charity
> Alack! and fie for shame!
> Young men will do't, if they come to't,
> By cock, they are to blame,
> Quoth she, before you tumbled me,
> You promised me to wed.

Here, *cock* is a disguised oath for *GOD*, but it is also intended as a bawdy pun.

JERK

(*col.*) *A fool or bore.*

This meaning seems to be derived from the American expression '*jerk off*' meaning to masturbate. A *jerk*, therefore, is somewhat akin to a *wanker*.

As a verb, the word was once used to mean 'flog'. The ideas of masturbation and violence are often associated in English. For example, masturbation is also known as *beating the meat*, *flogging the bishop*, *boxing the jesuit*, *galloping the maggot*, and *bashing the dummy*.

For additional colour the word *jerk* can be used in combinations such as *jerk the turkey*, and *jerk the gherkin*, both of which also refer to masturbation.

The expression to *jack off* appears to be simply a variation of to *jerk off*.

JEWELS

(col.) The genitals.

The male genitals are sometimes known as the *family jewels*, an expression which encapsulates both their value and their importance to future generations.

Shakespeare frequently used the word as a synonym for 'maidenhead' and hence virginity; and in China the clitoris is elegantly known as the *jewel terrace*.

JIG

(col.) Sexual intercourse.

The old adage that dancing is the perpendicular expression of a horizontal desire is reflected in a number of terms like this. Sexual intercourse is also known, for example, as a *blanket hornpipe*.

Variations on the simple word *jig* include *feather bed jig* and *buttock jig*. Others, employing reduplication, include *jiggy-jig*, *jigga-jig*, and *jig-jig*, this last partially repopularized by Graham Greene's *Travels with My Aunt*.

The word *gigolo*, translated from its native Italian, means literally 'jigger'.

JIMINY CRICKET!

(col.) An exclamation.

Like so many apparently meaningless exclamations this one disguises its original form. It is a variation of *Jiminy Christmas!*, itself a euphemism for *Jesus Christ*. See OATH.

JIMMY RIDDLE

(col.) The act of urinating.

This is Cockney rhyming slang, the rhyme being provided by the word *PIDDLE*.

JOB, ON THE

(*col.*) *Engaged in sexual intercourse.*

This phrase dates from the late nineteenth century, although it may be significant that as a verb the word *job* has an ancient meaning of 'prod' or 'thrust'.

An alternative explanation is that the phrase simply reflects a common association of sexual intercourse and physical work. In this context it is interesting to note how often the male genitals are likened to workmen's equipment (see TOOL).

JOEY

(*col.*) *A dupe or fool.*

In Cockney rhyming slang *Joey* is really *Joey Hunt*, a CUNT; hence a fool.

JOHN

(*col.*) *The penis (mainly UK), a lavatory (mainly US).*

For centuries, men's names have been attached to their penises. *John* is a good example of this habit, more common now in the fuller form *John Thomas*, which was popularized by D. H. Lawrence in *Lady Chatterley's Lover*. As well as variations of *John* such as *JOHNNEY* and *Jack*, names used in this way at various times include *Willy, Percy, Rupert, Peter, Mick, DICK*, and *ROGER*.

In America *john* is a slang term for a lavatory. The supplement to the *Oxford English Dictionary* quotes an early use of the word in the compound form *cuzjohn*, 'cousin john', from 1735 in relation to the rules at Harvard: 'No freshman shall mingo against the College wall or go into the fellow's cuzjohn'.

It is possible that puritan Americans started using the word in this sense, regarding it as a euphemism for *JAKES*, which they would have regarded as improper.

JOHNNEY

(col.) A contraceptive sheath.

This is a contraction of the term *johnney bag*. Since the word *JOHN* is an old slang term for the penis, a *johnney bag* was literally a bag for the penis.

To emphasize the distinction between *johnney* meaning penis, and *johnney* meaning contraceptive sheath, we still often refer to the latter specifically as a *rubber johnney*.

K

KARSY

(*col.*) *See* LAVATORY.

KHYBER

(*col.*) *The anus.*

This is Cockney rhyming slang. The full form is *Khyber Pass*, . rhyming with *ARSE*.

KISS MY ARSE

(*col.*) *An expression of contempt.*

The act of kissing another's arse symbolizes an extremely abject status. It was, for example, once commonly believed that at sabbats witches would kiss the Devil's arse as part of their self-debasing ritual.

The principle was familiar to Shakespeare. In *The Second Part of Henry VI* (IV. vii. 31) the fawning French Dauphin is referred to as *Monsier Basimecu*, the name being a pun on the French *baise mon cul*, literally 'kiss-my-arse'.

The association between fawning and the performance of unappealing acts is reflected in a number of expressions, for further examples see SUCKHOLE.

In the *1811 Dictionary of the Vulgar Tongue*, under the heading '*kiss mine arse*', is the observation 'An offer . . . very frequently made, but never . . . literally accepted'. The position has not changed much since then.

Many of the best English proverbs have traditionally been omitted from reference books because of their indelicate nature. One such, noted by Eric Partridge and presumably used by pragmatic ladies, was 'He that doth kiss and do no more, may kiss behind and not before'.

For reasons which are, unfortunately, lost to history there are a number of place names in Cheshire which make reference to arse kissing. Examples are *Kiss Arse Hill* at Rainow, and *Kiss Arse Wood* at Wincle.

KNACKER

(col.) As a noun, a testicle; as a verb, to tire or exhaust.

The common theme between these apparently unconnected meanings is provided by an old association between testicles and strength. Thus, to *knacker* was originally to geld, to cut off an animal's *knackers*. A gelded animal loses its virility and becomes markedly more docile; in a sense it is weakened. The expression to *knacker* therefore acquired a secondary meaning of 'to weaken', so to be *knackered* is to be 'exhausted'. Once weak and exhausted, working animals tend not to live long – they are slaughtered. This establishes a further link between *knackers' yards* and slaughterhouses.

The association between testicles and power is ancient and well attested in English. For other examples see SPUNK.

KNEE TREMBLER, A

(col.) Sexual intercourse while standing.

First recorded around 1850, this phrase is currently enjoying new popularity.

It refers to the involuntary leg movements which are characteristic of this variety of intercourse.

Knickers

Women's underpants.

This word is guaranteed to raise a laugh amongst the especially vacuous. Its power to amuse is a direct result of its recent status as a semi-taboo word, underwear being regarded as too suggestive of what might be found underneath.

Knickers is a contraction of *knickerbockers*, a term originally applied to breeches gathered at the knee. It was adapted from the Dutch name *Knickerbocker*, which belonged to the fictitious author of *A History of New York* (actually written by Washington Irving in 1809). Illustrations for the book showed the townsmen wearing characteristic Dutch baggy trousers.

In the USA, golfing breeches are still sometimes known as *knickers*. In England such breeches are generally worn four inches longer than conventional knickers, and are therefore known as *plus fours*.

Knob

(col.) The penis head, more generally the penis.

One of the words for the penis which reflect a visual resemblance (see ACORN).

As a slang term, before the late nineteenth century, *knob* generally meant simply 'head'.

Knock

(col.) To copulate with a woman.

This usage dates from the sixteenth century at least. Nowadays the word is generally found in combinations such as *knock off* and *knock up*, this latter sometimes being used to mean 'to make pregnant'.

In Britain, the expression to *knock up* also has a non-sexual meaning – to wake up by making a knocking noise. This meaning is not widely known in the USA and consequently a certain amount of transcontinental misunderstanding has been known to occur.

Knock is one of the numerous words for copulation which also have violent connotations (see BONK).

We still occasionally call brothels *knocking shops*, but nightgowns are no longer called *knocking jackets*, as they once were, when all decent folk slept naked.

KNOCKERS

(col.) The female breasts.

Although the word *knocker* has enjoyed a variety of slang meanings over the centuries, this one was not recorded before the 1940s.

The word, first noted in the USA, sounds remarkably similar to the Australian expression *norkers*, which has exactly the same meaning (see NORK). The fact that the Australian expression had already gained international popularity before the American form appeared suggests that *knockers* may simply be a corruption of it. (Slang travels very quickly in wartime, the armed forces being efficient vectors for spreading it. The corruption would be fairly natural, since the significance of the term *norkers* would not be recognized in the USA.)

KNOW

To have sexual intercourse with.

Often, to make the meaning clear, the word is qualified with 'in the Biblical sense'. The translators of the Old Testament used *know* because the corresponding Hebrew word had the same dual meaning.

One consequence of this usage is the inevitable ambiguity which occasionally arises. Sometimes the word merely means to be acquainted with.

The following passage from Genesis (14: 5) has given the Sodomites such a bad reputation; they have seen two messengers visit Lot's house during the previous night:

And they called unto Lot, and said unto him,
Where are the men which came to thee in the night?
Bring them out unto us, that we may know them.

The pious Lot declined, but offered to let them know two of his daughters instead.

L

LABIA

The lips of the female genitals.

In Latin the word *labium* means lip, so the lips of the female genitals are technically the *labia pudenda*, the outer ones are the *labia majora*, the inner the *labia minora*.

In 1722, Quincey referred to them in a medical reference book[6] as 'The labia, or Lips of the great Chink'.

LATRINE

See LAVATORY.

LAVATORY

A place set aside for excretion.

It is curious that the English language has no single accepted word for this facility. *Lavatory* is probably the nearest we have to one. With the honourable exceptions of a few terms like *shit house*, most of our words for it are euphemisms. Generally, these euphemisms reduce to the following broad categories – 'a place with running water', 'a dirty place', 'a small or private place', and 'a place of need or easement'.

In Anglo-Saxon times a favourite word was *gang*, meaning 'a place to go' (our modern *gang* is related, it denotes a group of people who go about together; and in northern British dialects the verb *gang* is

---

[6] *Lexicon Physico-medicum*, 2nd Edn., p. 174 (1722).

still used to mean to go). To be explicit one could refer to an *earsgang*, literally an 'arse-go'.

By Chaucer's time *gang* had been joined by several other terms. One of them, *privy* 'a private place', was Standard English for centuries and is still well known. In this passage from *The Merchant's Tale* (E 1953–4) the young bride disposes of a letter from her lover:

> She rent it all to clouts at last
> And in the privy softly it cast.

Another Chaucerian term is *wardrobe*, a typical example from the 'small or private place' category. In *The Prioress's Tale* (B2 572–3) a boy is murdered and his body thrown into a privy:

> I say that in a wardrobe they him slew
> Where these Jews purge their entrails.

This word is essentially a French variation of the Norman French *garderobe*, a term still used in English as a technical name for the type of primitive lavatory found in ancient castles.

More terms had come into use by Shakespeare's time. Amongst them were *BOG(S)*, *JAKES*, and *DUNNY*, all of which are still in use in various places around the world today. Another expression was *stool*, short for *stool of ease* or *close stool*; originally the term denoted what we would now call a *commode* but later extended its meaning to include other types of privy. Even today the expression *at stool* is used to mean 'excreting', and we have now further extended the meaning so that a turd may be called a *stool*.

Also dating from the seventeenth century is the word *latrine*, from the Latin *latrina* with the same meaning. The Latin word was derived from *lavatrina*, which denoted a place for washing. Around the same time we also find terms such as *necessary house*, *gingerbread office*, and *closet of ease*. This use of the word *closet* closely parallels the earlier *wardrobe*.

In the eighteenth century the *closet* became a *water closet*. Alternatively, it could be a *house of office*, a *temple of cloacina*, a *cackatorium* (see CACK), or rather coyly a *little house*. Also around this time the word *heads* is first recorded. A naval term, it originally denoted part of a sailing ship near the bows which overhung the sea. Only a grating separated sailors from the water so waste disposal of various types was relatively easy there.

As might be expected, the nineteenth century saw the introduction of more evasive names. Even the already euphemistic *water closet* became an anonymous *W.C.* It is a reflection of Britain's international influence during Victorian times that the letters W.C. may still be seen on lavatory doors throughout the world.

The nineteenth century also saw the introduction of the euphemistic *convenience* and *toilet*. Based on the French *toilette*, this latter originally denoted a small cloth laid on a dressing table. To be *at one's toilet* was to be preparing oneself in private. Indeed, this suggestion of private preparation is preserved in our use of the term *toileteries*, and in particular the expression *toilet soap*, which tends to conjure up unedifying thoughts in children's minds.

Although it has been in use since the fourteenth century to denote a place for washing, the word *lavatory* has been used in its current sense only since the twentieth century. The word quickly gained popularity to become what was regarded as the proper word, and *toilet* came to be regarded as rather vulgar. In England the signs on public lavatories often reflect the social status of the area: *Ladies'* and *Gentlemen's lavatories* are the most prestigious, *Public Conveniences* are blatantly middle class, *Ladies'* and *Gents' Toilets* are decidedly down-market. *Men* and *Women* are intended to be modern and trendy and are therefore also down-market, as are other possibilities (*guys'* and *dolls'*, *stags'* and *does'*, *Jack* and *Jill*, etc.).

In speech, the word *toilet* has recently been gaining status. In England the upper classes have started to adopt it out of perversity, the suburban middle classes having finally taken to the 'U' *lavatory*.

However, the words *lav* and *lavvy* are still most definitely 'non-U'. So is *karzy*, a corruption of the euphemistic Italian *casa*, meaning 'house'.

Recently, the social pattern has also been complicated by the word *loo*. Originally an upper-class word it has now become common. It is apparently derived from the name of Lady Louise Hamilton. The story is that when she was staying at the vice-regal lodge in Dublin around 1870, the name card on her bedroom door was transferred to the lavatory door. The card had read simply '*Lou*' and the joke was immortalized by the other guests who persisted in referring to the lavatory as *lou*. As the expression gained popularity amongst those who did not know its origin the usual spelling was changed to *loo*.

Australians, like the British upper and lower classes, have traditionally taken a positive pleasure in discussing lavatorial matters.

Hence the free use of terms such as *crap house*, *shit house*, and *thunder box*. Field latrines were apparently dubbed *thunder boxes*, not only for the obvious reason, but also because of the unfortunate phenomena caused by users throwing cigarette ends into them and igniting the highly explosive methane gas generated there.

The British middle classes and Americans, on the other hand, are traditionally embarrassed by lavatorial matters, and prefer extreme and absurd euphemisms. In suburban England the lavatory might be called a *whatsit*, a *youknow*, the *powder room*, the *little girl's* or *boy's room*, the *cloakroom*, the *smallest room in the house*, the *geography of the house* (as in 'Let me show you *the geography of the house*'), or the *euphemism* (as in 'I'm just going to the *euphemism*'). In the USA it is a *bathroom*, a *washroom*, a *rest room*, or, most preposterously, a *comfort station*.

More direct American terms include *can* and *john*, though even *JOHN* is probably a euphemism for *JAKES*.

LAY

(*col.*) *To copulate with. See* LIE WITH.

LEAK

(*col.*) *To urinate.*

This is an old euphemism. It was well known to Shakespeare: in *The First Part of Henry IV* (II. i. 19–21) a servant complains about not having a chamber pot, or as he calls it a jordan: 'Why, they will allow us ne'er a jordan, and then we leak in the chimney . . .'.

LEG OVER, TO GET ONE'S

(*col.*) *To copulate, usually said of men rather than women.*

This phrase follows an ancient tradition by which activities with the legs were associated with sexual activity. Thus, sexual intercourse was also known as *lifting one's leg*, *laying one's leg over*, or simply *leg business*.

85

In *Othello* (III. iii. 424–5) Shakespeare makes Iago report Cassio's fictitious misbehaviour whilst asleep '. . . Then he laid his leg over my thigh, and sigh'd and kiss'd'.

LESBIAN

A female homosexual.

The word originally meant 'pertaining to Lesbos'. Lesbos being a Greek island where Sappho, a renowned poetess and lesbian, lived around 600 BC.

Because of Sappho's dual claims to fame, the adjective *sapphic* may be applied both to a type of poetic metre, and also to lesbian activities.

LIE WITH

To copulate with.

This is an ancient euphemism, and one favoured by the translators of the King James' Bible. According to Exodus 12: 16, for example, '. . . if a man entice a maid that is not betrothed, and lie with her; he shall surely endow her to be his wife'.

Shakespeare also used the expression. King Edward speaking to Lady Grey in *The Third Part of Henry VI* (III. ii. 69) says: 'To tell thee plain, I aim to lie with thee'. Again, in *Othello* (IV. i. 34–5):

IAGO. Lie—
OTHELLO. With her?
IAGO. With her, on her; what you will.
OTHELLO. Lie with her! Lie on her!

Confusion between the verbs *lie* and *lay*, now endemic throughout the English speaking world, has resulted in the use of the expression to *lay* meaning to copulate with.

As Dorothy Parker observed 'If all the girls attending it [the Yale prom] were laid end to end, I wouldn't be at all surprised'.

LINGAM

The penis.

This is a Sanskrit word meaning 'the sign of the male'. It is the masculine counterpart of the feminine YONI.

Words such as these are used in English because they avoid the pejorative associations of native words, and the clinical formality of Latin ones.

LITTLE MAN IN A BOAT

(col.) The clitoris.

This is a reference to the fancied visual similarity. The metaphor parallels an ancient Roman one. In Latin the word *navicula* meant 'boat', and *naviculans* 'clitoris'.

LOBCOCK

(col.) A large flaccid penis.

The word is also a conventional term for a slow or stupid person, but it has had its secondary sexual meaning since at least the eighteenth century.

LOO

(col.) See LAVATORY.

M

MAKE LOVE

To copulate.

Not so very long ago this phrase meant 'to woo' or 'pay court', but within the last twenty years it has gained favour as the genteel euphemism which it now is.

The relatively recent shift of meaning often leaves the younger generation confused when they hear the term used in books, plays and films from before the 1960s. The change occurred at roughly the same time that the phrase 'make love not war' first became popular, a correspondence which may not be altogether coincidental.

As so often, Shakespeare seems to have anticipated the modern usage. In the following passage Hamlet is painting a less than attractive picture of his mother's relationship with her new husband: '. . . but to live in the rank sweat on an unseamed bed, stew'd in corruption, honeying and making love . . .' (*Hamlet* [III. iv. 94]).

MAMMARIES

(col.) The female breasts.

The term is short for *mammary glands*, which is exactly what the female breasts are. Mammary glands are so called from the Latin *mamma* meaning breast.

The Latin word also appears in *mammal*: a mammal is an animal which suckles its young.

Ultimately, words like *mamma* are based on the first vocal noises that babies make. Many languages, whether related or not, have words like *mamma*, *babba*, and *pappa* to denote babies, parents, or breasts (see also P A P).

MARBLES

(*col.*) *Testicles.*

This is one of many slang terms for the testicles which refer to their approximately spherical shape (see BALLS). In this case the reference is to the little balls, originally made of marble, which are used in the well-known children's game.

The phrase '*he hasn't got all his marbles*' originally referred to the testicles. In recent times, however, the idea of being not quite all there has been transferred from physical to mental faculties.

MASTURBATION

Manual sexual stimulation, generally of one's own body.

Traditionally this activity has been regarded as, and explicitly known as, *self-abuse* or *self-pollution*. Indeed, the very word *masturbation* is composed of Latin elements which reflect the idea of defiling with the hand. The two elements correspond to *manu-*, meaning 'hand', and *stuprare*, 'to defile'.

MENSTRUATION

See CURSE.

MERKIN

A pubic wig.

These items still exist, although they are not so much in demand as they were in previous centuries. They were especially popular when the usual treatment for venereal disease involved shaving off the pubic hair.

The word is a variation of *Malkin*. Though it is now little used, it was a common female name for over a thousand years.

Although the word is not as well known as it once was, it is far from obsolete. In the film *Dr Strangelove* the name of the president of the USA was chosen with some care; he was called *Merkin Muffley*.

METTLE

(*col.*) *Semen*.

Standard English meanings of the word include 'temperament', 'courage', and 'spirited disposition'. The colloquial meaning exactly parallels that of SPUNK, a word which also has a standard meaning of 'courage'.

In *Henry V* (III. v. 27–31) the Dauphin complains:

> By faith and honour,
> Our madams mock at us, and plainly say
> Our mettle is bred out and they will give
> Their bodies to the lust of English youth
> To new-store France with bastard warriers.

Etymologically the word is identical to *metal*, the two spellings being used interchangeably until the last century. Up until then the phrase to *fetch metal*, applied to men, meant to masturbate.

MICKEY, TO TAKE THE

(*col.*) *To ridicule*.

Here *Mickey* is Cockney rhyming slang, the full form being *Mickey Bliss*, meaning *piss*. To *take the Mickey*, or *Michael*, is, therefore, to *take the piss*.

MINGE

(*col.*) *The female genitals*.

The word is not recorded before 1903, but the fact that it was then a dialect term suggests that it is much older.

Its development is obscure, but one possibility is that it was borrowed from the Romanies who use a similar term.

MISTRESS

A kept woman.

In standard English the word *mistress* is the female counterpart of the male *master*, but it has had this secondary sexual connotation for centuries. Shakespeare's usage is sometimes ambiguous, though the King James' Bible consistently uses the word in its conventional sense.

Recent sensitivity has caused the word to be avoided, however innocent its use. Thus, for example, one of the teachers' unions is called the National Association of Schoolmasters and Union of Women Teachers rather than, say, the Union of School Masters and Mistresses.

The title *mistress* was long ago abbreviated to either *Miss* or *Mrs*, and recently also to *Ms*. As in earlier centuries, women generally adopt the form *Mrs* when they marry. In the past, however, spinsters of a certain age would also adopt the title. It signified the owner's status, whether acquired through marriage or age. The same sort of thing still happens elsewhere in Europe: for example in Germany a middle-aged *Fräulein* will spontaneously transmute into a *Frau*, and in France a *Mademoiselle* will change into a *Madame*.

MONOSYLLABLE, THE

(col.) The female genitals.

The word is an old euphemism for CUNT. It was popular in the early nineteenth century but dates from much earlier.

The meaning presumably developed from usage such as that of Lucas who, in *The Gamesters* (1714), wrote of '. . . a bawdy monosyllable such as boys write upon walls'.

MONS VENERIS

A woman's pubic mound.

This is a Latin term for the fleshy pubic region usually covered by the pubic hair. It translates literally as the mount or mound of Venus.

The term is also used by palmists, but to them it denotes the raised fleshy part of the palm at the base of the thumb.

MOON

(*col.*) *To exhibit the buttocks.*

Apparently coined only in the 1960s, the term clearly refers to the visual similarity between rounded buttocks and the moon. As an insulting gesture, however, the practice has been known for centuries.

The ancient practice of mooning regained popularity when the authorities started to take a harder line on streaking. The advantage of mooning is presumably that it can be stopped very quickly.

MOTHER

(*col.*) *A term of abuse.*

When used in this way the term is short for *mother fucker*, an expression which draws its effect from the powerful taboo concerning incest.

Prohibitions on incest provide our most rational sexual restrictions. Such restrictions make a great deal of evolutionary sense and are therefore found in many societies, even amongst animals. The only curious aspect is that there are so few taboo words for the subject in English.

Mount

To copulate with (of men).

This term dates back at least to the sixteenth century when it was Standard English and was used of both men and male animals. It refers specifically to the position generally adopted by animals for sexual intercourse.

For other words for copulation which have animal associations see TUP.

Muff

(col.) The female genitals.

Apparently the word originally referred specifically to the pubic hair, but it has been used in this sense since the seventeenth century at least. In the 1699 *New Dictionary of the Canting Crew* it was defined as 'a woman's secrets'. The word is also used as a synonym for *prostitute*.

Cunnilingus is sometimes called *muff-diving*.

N

NAFF

(col.) A term of contempt; hence naff-off, *an uncompromising instruction to go away.*

In the last century the word had a more precise meaning: it was one of the many names for the vagina.

It is apparently a euphemism, its Anglo-Saxon precursor *nafala* having meant 'navel'. (In fact the modern word *navel* is derived from *nafala*.)

For no very good reason the navel has often been associated with the genitals, and even today names for the navel are used as euphemisms for the genitals. (See for example the Behemoth quotation at STONES.) The contemplation of one's navel by Hindus is a substitute for the contemplation of Vishnu's navel, an activity connected to worship of the YONI, or female genitals.

NAKEDNESS

In the King James' Bible references to uncovering nakedness are often euphemisms for some sort of sexual activity.

In Leviticus (18: 6–20) there are numerous instructions about whose nakedness one is not allowed to uncover. In the following sample (verses 8–10) the references appear to be to conventional sexual intercourse:

The nakedness of thy father's wife shalt thou not uncover: it is thy father's nakedness.

The nakedness of thy sister, the daughter of thy father, or daughter of thy mother, whether she be born at home, or born abroad, even their nakedness thou shalt not uncover.

The nakedness of thy son's daughter, or of thy daughter's daughter, even their nakedness thou shalt not uncover: for their's is thine own nakedness.

In Genesis (9: 20–4), however, the reference is more obscure:

And Noah began to be an husbandman, and he planted a vineyard. And he drank of the wine, and was drunken; and he was uncovered within his tent.

And Ham, the father of Canaan, saw the nakedness of his father, and told his two brethren without.

And Shem and Japheth took a garment, and laid it upon both their shoulders, and went backward, and covered the nakedness of their father; and their faces were backward, and they saw not their father's nakedness.

And Noah awoke from his wine, and knew what his younger son had done to him.

According to Rabinical authorities the implication is that Ham either castrated Noah, or 'indulged a peverted lust upon him'.

Elsewhere in the King James' Bible the translators used the explicit phrase to '*go into*' to refer to men having sexual intercourse. In more recent translations the phraseology ranges from the bland '*have intercourse with*' (New English Bible) to the coy '*sleep with*' (Jerusalem Bible).

NAUGHTY

(*col.*) *Immoral, smutty, obscene.*

This word's association with sex is a very old one. It is clear in Shakespeare's use (see, for example, the quotation at COME). In *Measure For Measure* (II. i. 75–6) it is apparent that a *naughty house* is a brothel.

Like the standard meaning of the adjective *naughty*, the colloquial one is a development of its earlier sense of 'worthless'. Indeed the word's form reflects its original meaning of 'worth *naught*'.

The word may also be used as a noun, as in the Australian phrase to *have a naughty*, meaning to have sexual intercourse. In England, however, one generally *does a naughty*, although this can cover virtually any activity not generally appreciated in public.

NAVEL

See NAFF.

NIPPLE

A teat.

The word has a more general meaning and may be applied to any small projection with an orifice. Nipples feature heavily in engineering, where they are used for such purposes as regulating fluid flow and lubricating machinery.

In origin, *nipple* is a diminutive of *nib*, a word denoting any projecting point, as for example a pen nib.

NOOKEY

(*col.*) *Sexual intercourse, sometimes a* bit of nookey.

This sense seems to date only from the early years of this century. In recent years the expression has sometimes been extended to produce forms such as *nookey push-push*, which tend to enjoy fleeting popularity, especially in the USA.

The origin of the expression is not known. One possible explanation is that it is related to the word *nook*, a slang term for the female genitals (see CRACK).

NORK

(*col.*) *A female breast.*

This term is derived from the name of the *Norco Co-operative Ltd*, an Australian butter manufacturer based in New South Wales. Norco butter advertisements at one time featured a picture of a cow with an unusually prominent udder. Initially the word was used in joking reference to this famous udder.

The term gained international currency during the First World War and has since lost and regained popularity on both sides of the world. Not surprisingly, it is usually found in its plural form *norks*, also as *norkers*, *norgs* or *norgers* (see also KNOCKERS).

Breast fondling is occasionally referred to as *norging*.

NORMA SNOCKERS

(*col.*) *Large breasts.*

This humorous expression is presumably a corruption of *enormous knockers* deliberately fashioned to resemble a woman's name. In this it is comparable to GERT STONKERS.

NUBILE

(*col.*) *Attractive* (*used only of young women*).

This usage results from a misunderstanding about the conventional meaning which is 'marriageable'. In fact the word is derived from the Latin *nubere*, meaning 'to marry'.

Also related are the words *connubial* and *nuptial*, both of which are still associated with marriage, and also *NYMPH*, a word of Greek origin which shares the same ultimate root.

Nunnery

(*col.*) *A brothel.*

The term is not as popular now as it was in Elizabethan times when nuns had more dubious reputations than they do now.

When Hamlet says to Ophelia 'Get thee to a nunnery' (*Hamlet* [III. i. 124]) it is clear from the context that he is using the word in this sense.

Nut

(*col.*) *Testicle.*

In earlier times the conventional type of nut was rare and valuable, so the word was naturally applied to any delightful object. We still use the expression *as sweet as a nut*, despite the introduction of refined sugar.

Testicles have been called *nuts* only in recent times. When used in this way the term is apparently a shortened version of *nutmegs*, this form having been used to mean testicles since the seventeenth century.

Long before then *nut* had had an alternative sexual meaning (see ACORN).

Nymph

(*col.*) *A sexually available attractive young woman.*

This usage is founded on two popular misconceptions. One is the assumption that the word is a contraction of *nymphomaniac*. The other is a misunderstanding about the nature of nymphomania (see NYMPHO).

The conventional meaning of *nymph*, carried over from the original Greek, is 'maiden' or 'bride'. In Ancient Greek the word was applied to certain beautiful young demi-goddesses whose virginity was perpetually renewed.

The inner lips of the female genitals, the *labia minora*, are alternatively known as the *nymphae*.

Etymologically, *nymph* is closely related to *NUBILE*, a word which has attracted similar misunderstandings in English.

NYMPHET

A sexually attractive young girl.

Revived by Vladimir Nabokov in his 1958 novel *Lolita*, this word has since gained wide currency.

The term *lolita* is used in much the same way, *Lolita* being the name of the principal nymphet in Nabokov's novel.

NYMPHO

(*col.*) *A promiscuous woman with prodigious sexual appetites.*

The term is applied to women who exist more in men's fantasies rather than the real world.

It is based on the word *nymphomaniac*, a technical term for a woman suffering from a medical condition involving morbid and uncontrollable sexual desires.

O

O

A representation of the female genitals.

This is one of many terms which liken the vagina to a sort of ring.
See CIRCLE for other examples.

Shakespeare used it with bawdy overtones in many of his plays.
Indeed its use is a good indicator of where his suggestive puns are
the densest. Many of the Shakespearian quotations in this book, for
example, include it.

OATH

A call upon supernatural forces for assistance.

In the Western world taboos are mostly associated with sex and
excretion, but in previous centuries they usually made reference to
some sort of imaginary supernatural being. To a much reduced
extent any trivial mention of God is still regarded as somehow improper (see GOD).

The ostensible reason for avoiding the name of God is that the
swearing of oaths is prohibited in the Bible. In fact Biblical injunc-
tions are ambiguous or contradictory, so that different Christian
groups disagree about what is permissible. Some Christians will not
even swear the usual oath used in courts of law 'I promise to tell the
truth, the whole truth, and nothing but the truth, so help me God'.

Being resourceful, people over the centuries have developed a
number of ways of getting round prohibitions on oaths. One way is
to contract the expression incorporating the awful name so that it
becomes unrecognizable (see GADZOOKS, STRUTH, DRAT
IT, ZOUNDS, and GOR BLIMEY, all of which contain re-

sidual contractions of *God*). Another favoured method is to use an expression in which the sound of the prohibited word is used, but not the word itself. Thus the name *God* can be conveniently spoken as part of exclamations such as *Gordon Bennet!* and *Gordon Highlanders!* Yet another method is to distort the name itself beyond recognition, thus we have totally meaningless words like *GOLLY!* and *GOSH!*

Such bizarre convolutions are not confined to English. The French for example have a favourite exclamation *sacre bleu!*, 'holy blue!', a corruption of *sacre dieu!*, 'holy God!'.

God is not the only name tabooed in this way. Another family of oaths for example incorporate the name *Jesus*. Common acceptable variations of this name include *GEE!*, *GEE-WHIZZ!*, and *JEEZE!*; *Christ!* becomes *cripes!*, *crikey!*, or *criminy!*; and the full *Jesus Christ!* becomes *JEEPERS CREEPERS!* or even *JIMINY CRICKET!*

In this book such evasions are referred to as *disguised oaths*. They are also known as *minced oaths* or *shunt words*.

See also SWEAR-WORD.

ONANISM

Masturbation.

Though still in limited use, the term is not as popular as it was in Victorian times. It was coined around the beginning of the eighteenth century, the first record of its use being in a cyclopedia where it was described as a term 'which some late empirics have framed, to denote the crime of self pollution'.

The term is modelled on the name of *Onan*, a biblical character who was once regarded as the first documented wanker. The relevant passage is found in the book of Genesis (38: 8–10). Judah's firstborn has just been slain by God who did not approve of him. Onan is another son of Judah, and therefore brother to the dead man:

And Judah said unto Onan, go in unto thy brother's wife, and marry her, and raise up seed to thy brother.

And Onan knew that the seed should not be his; and it came to pass, when he went in unto his brother's wife, that he spilled it on

the ground, lest that he should give seed to his brother.
And the thing which he did displeased the Lord; wherefor he slew him also.

(In Biblical use *SEED* is used to mean both 'offspring' and 'semen'.)

This passage provided the grounds for Christian condemnation of masturbation throughout the centuries. It is not clear, however, whether God was displeased with Onan because he had been masturbating, or because he had declined to follow his father's instructions. More serious still, it is not certain that the spilling of seed involved masturbation at all. Onan might equally well have been practising *coitus interruptus*.

Knowing the above passage, a number of parrot owners (including Dorothy Parker) called their birds *Onan* because, like their biblical namesake, they are given to spilling their seed on the ground.

ONE-EYED TROUSER SNAKE

(*col.*) *The penis.*

This is one of a number of humorous expressions for the penis which have been developed in Australia and exported to the UK since the 1950s.

The phallic associations of snakes are well established in many cultures, and indeed feature heavily in various kinds of psycho-analysis.

Even the monocular theme has been used before: a rather dated and academic joke is to refer to a penis as *Polyphemus*. The original Polyphemus was a one-eyed giant, the King of the Cyclops killed by Odysseus in Homer's *Odyssey*.

ORCHESTRAS

(*col.*) *Testicles.*

This is a popular contraction of *orchestra stalls*, Cockney rhyming slang for *BALLS*.

An alternative slang term for *balls*, *COBBLERS* tends to be used when the reference is to *balls* meaning nonsense. *Orchestras* however is usually used when the reference really is to testicles.

Like all Cockney rhyming slang the expression's origin lies no earlier than the nineteenth century.

ORCHID

(col.) Testicle.

The term is now little used in this sense, the ancient connection between orchids and testicles having been conveniently forgotten.

Whether used to mean 'testicle' or as the name of a type of plant, *orchid* is fashioned after the Greek *orchis*, which also meant 'testicle'. (From it we also have the medical term *orchidectomy*, more correctly *orchiectomy*, denoting surgical castration.)

The plants known as *orchids* are so called because they have tubers shaped like testicles. Native English words for various types of orchid include *ballock grass*, *ballock wort*, *priest ballocks*, *hare's ballocks*, *fox ballocks*, and *sweet ballocks*. Other names also refer to testicles: for example, *CULLIONS* and *dogstones* (see STONES). *Dogstones* is a literal translation of the Latin name *testiculus canis*. In the sixteenth century orchids were actually called *testicles*.

The continuing use of orchids as love tokens is not altogether unconnected with their traditional association with testicles.

ORGAN

(col.) The genitals (usually male).

This sense is merely a special case of a more general meaning: 'instrument', 'implement', or 'TOOL'. It has developed from expressions such as *organs of generation*. Although usually applied to male genitals, the term can be applied to female genitals. Shakespeare, for example, in *King Lear* (I. iv. 284–7) refers to *organs of increase*:

> Into her womb convey sterility!
> Dry up in her the organs of increase;
> And from her derogate body never spring
> A babe to honour her.

The word is used in many other spheres: we speak, for example, of *vital organs* of the body, and of *organs of government*. With various degrees of seriousness it is also used of publications. In the following passage Lord Gnome employs a customary double entendre:

> The gorgeous pouting Rita Chevrolet (38–24–36) is taking on my organ and it's going to be a pleasure to serve under her!
>
> (*Private Eye* Editorial, 10 July 1987)

The *musical organ* is so called because it is exactly that: a musical instrument. This too provides scope for suggestive meanings. To *play one's organ* for example means to 'masturbate'. The basic idea is much the same as *playing the silent flute*, or *playing the pink oboe*.

P

PANDAR, OR PANDER

As a noun, one who procures sexual services for another; hence as a verb, to indulge another.

The word is derived from the name *Pandarus*, a character in the story of Troilus and Cressida who acts as a go-between. Boccaccio, Chaucer and Shakespeare are between them responsible for Pandarus' bad reputation: Homer's original Pandarus was not a pandar at all.

In his *Troilus and Cressida* (III. ii. 195–200) Shakespeare explicitly encourages the calumny by making Pandarus say to the two lovers:

> ... If ever you prove false to one another, since I have taken such pains to bring you together, let all pitiful goers between be call'd to the world's end after my name; call them all Pandars; let all inconstant men be Troiluses, all false women Cressidas, and all brokers between Pandars!

PAP

Anodyne entertainment.

This modern meaning is an extension of a much older one: soft food for infants, hence any easily digested mush or pulp. In turn this is an extension of the original meaning: a breast or teat, a source of milk for infants. Ultimately, the word is echoic; it mimics the lip smacking sounds of sucking babies.

Sensitivities about this and other words associated with breast feeding have changed over the centuries. Wyclif in his version of the Bible produced in the fourteenth century refers to *teetis*, i.e.

teats. Later versions however tend to favour *paps*; in the King James' Bible of 1611 for example Luke (11: 27) has an unnamed woman say to Jesus 'Blessed is the womb that bare thee, and the paps which thou hast sucked'. In the Revised Version of the 1880s however these *paps* became *breasts*.

Presumably because they are only secondary sexual organs the breasts have never been completely taboo. Associated words, therefore, although they may need to be used with care, do not generally become so unacceptable that they are driven out of use altogether. Terms primarily connected with sex on the other hand often disappear completely in the course of time. Once-common words like *SWIVE* and *PINTLE* are virtually unknown now. Their explicit sexual connotations have forced them out of use.

PECKER

(*US col.*) *The penis.*

In the UK this word generally means not 'penis', but 'nose'. It is liable, therefore, to transatlantic misunderstanding, especially in the expression *keep your pecker up*.

The American meaning has been known in certain circles in the UK for some time. For example, it is used in the song entitled 'The House Of The Rising Sun' popularized by the Animals in the 1960s. According to the *American Folk Music Occasional* (1,12,1964) the relevant words are:

> There is a house down in New Orleans,
> They call it The Rising Sun,
> When you want to get your pecker spoilt,
> That's where you get it done . . .

PEE

(*col.*) *As a noun, urine; as a verb, to urinate.*

The ancient word *PISS*, though it had served for centuries, was a little too direct for recent generations. One way of palliating the fancied offensiveness was to use initial letters instead of full words. Thus *piss* becomes *P*, pronounced 'pee', just as *bugger* became *B*, and *fuck* became *F*, still common in phrases such as *F-off* and *F'ing and blinding*.

PENIS

The male member or membrum virile.

This is a Latin word popularized in the mid eighteenth century when there was a large move towards the adoption of obscure classical terms. In ancient Rome the word penis had been used in the same way that it is now used in English, but ironically it was then regarded as slang. The original standard Latin meaning of the word was 'tail'.

As Cicero observed over two thousand years ago:

> Our ancestors called a tail a *penis*, and a paint brush is called a *penicillus* because it is like a tail; but now *penis* has become an indecent word.[7]

(From the diminutive form comes the modern English *penicillin*, the name of a mould whose sporangia resemble small paint brushes. The word *pencil* shares the same origin, denoting as it originally did a small paint brush.)

The original English term for the penis had been *PINTLE*, though this had already been joined by a string of alternatives such as *TAIL*, *TARSE*, *COCK*, *PRICK*, and *YARD*. (See also STICK, TOOL, JOHN, and WEAPON.)

Disliking the clinical formality of Latin terms and the extreme informality of native English ones, popular sayings often avoid both. The following piece of folk wisdom manages to be unambiguous, though its subject is never actually mentioned.

> Long and thin
> Goes right in
> But doesn't please the ladies,
> Short and thick
> Does the trick
> And gives them all the babies.

[7] Quoted by Jasper Griffin in *Fair of Speech* (see Bibliography).

Like the English, the French have a number of informal words for the penis. Some of the more common ones are *la queue* (the tail), *la verge* (the rod), *la bitte* (the bollard), *le zob*, and *la pine*.

PIDDLE

(*col.*) *As a noun, urine; as a verb, to urinate.*

Principally a children's word, it was first recorded with this sense in the late eighteenth century. *Piddling*, in the sense of trifling or petty is, however, much older. Samuel Johnson defined the verb as follows:

(1) To pick at table; to feed squeamishly, and without appetite . . .

(2) To trifle; to attend to small parts rather than the main . . .

The fact that no written record has survived for the urination sense from before the late eighteenth century does not, of course, prove that the word was not previously used in speech in this way. For one thing, a whole family of similar words including *paddle*, *puddle*, and *poodle*, have associated etymologies involving water, a fact which suggests that *piddle* may also be related.

In Dorset there is a *River Piddle*, along which may be found towns such as *Piddletrenthide*, *Piddlehinton*, *Puddletown*, *Tolpuddle*, *Affpuddle* and *Briantspuddle*, which show that the words *piddle* and *puddle* were virtually interchangeable.

Furthermore there are a number of field names in Berkshire and elsewhere which give similar clues. Waterlogged fields would often be given names such as *Piddle Meadow*.

PIECE

(*col.*) *A sexually attractive girl or woman.*

This usage dates back to the fourteenth century at least. It is sometimes made more explicit in compounds such as *piece of flesh*, *piece of arse*, *piece of crumpet*, *piece of skirt*, and *piece of tail*.

The *1811 Dictionary of the Vulgar Tongue* defines *piece* concisely as 'a wench'.

PILES

Haemorrhoids, small swellings around the anus.

This type of pile is named from the Latin *pila*, a ball; piles being roughly spherical in shape.

The word has nothing to do with *pile* meaning stake (as in *pile driver*), which has an entirely different etymology.

PILL

(col.) Testicle.

Like *PILES*, this word is derived from the Latin *pila*, meaning a ball. It is one of numerous colloquial terms for the testicles which make reference to their approximately spherical shape (see BALLS).

Other round objects are called *pills* for the same reason. Amongst the most common are small round tablets, and billiard and tennis balls.

PILLICOCK

(obs.) The penis.

Although the word is obsolete it has contributed to the creation of a new word, PILLOCK.

The first quotation under the heading *pillicock* given in the *Oxford English Dictionary* is dated as the early thirteen hundreds, and clearly uses the word in the sense of penis: 'Mi pilkoc pisseth on mi scone' ('my pillicock pisses on my shoes').

In Shakespeare's *King Lear* (III. iv. 74–5) Poor Tom's idiot ramblings include the line 'Pillicock sat on Pillicock Hill'. This apparently senseless observation is marginally less so given that *Pillicock* means penis, and *Pillicock Hill* refers to the female genitals.

PILLOCK

(*col.*) *Testicle.*

This term dates only from the nineteenth century, and seems to be a confused blend of two of its synonyms, *PILL* and *BALLOCK*. More recently it has come to be applied, like many other words with sexual connotations, to fools and incompetents.

Contributing to the nineteenth-century confusion surrounding the word's creation was another colloquial word, *PILLICOCK*, meaning 'penis', which had been in slang use since at least the fourteenth century.

PILLOW BITER

(*col.*) *A passive male homosexual.*

The expression is relatively recent in origin, apparently dating only from the 1970s.

It was probably suggested by some of the evidence given by Norman Scott in the widely reported trial of Jeremy Thorpe.

PIMP

A procurer.

The word has always had this meaning since it was first recorded in the early seventeenth century.

An entry in Pepys' Diary for 10 June 1666 notes with disfavour that 'The Duke of York is wholly given up to his new mistress . . . Mr Brouncker, it seems, was the pimp to bring it about'.

The word is probably adapted from a French word *pimper* meaning to dress well, but also to allure or seduce.

PINTLE

The penis.

Once Standard English, this term is now confined to dialect. In Scotland and the north of England it has survived longer than elsewhere. In some areas a prostitute might still be called a *pintle-bit*, *pintle maid*, *pintle fancier*, *pintle ranger*, *pintle merchant*, or *pintle monger*. So too, venereal disease might be called *pintle fever* or *pintle blossom*, and a lascivious leer be described as a *pintle keek*.

Lords and ladies, the common wild arum often found in hedgerows, glories in a number of alternative names which make reference to its long penis-like flower spike. One especially popular one is *cuckoo-pint*, short for *cuckoo pintle*, which originally meant something like 'lively penis'. Other names for it include *wake pintle*, *cuckoo cock*, *dog's cock*, *dog's dibble*, *dog's tausel*, and *dog's spear*.

P. H. Reaney in his book *The Origin of English Surnames* notes a number of obsolete surnames incorporating the word *pintle*. Amongst the owners of such names were *Robert Pintel* (1179), *Hugo Humpintel* (1187), *Alan Coltepyntel* (1275), *John Swetpintel* (1275) and *William Doggepintel* (1361).

PISS

(col.) As a verb, to urinate; as a noun, urine.

The word is not Anglo-Saxon despite its four letters. It is of French origin, and ultimately is almost certainly echoic: in other words it sounds like the characteristic noise of urination. It was Standard English from the Middle Ages up until the last century.

Chaucer used the word freely. The following passage from the *Wife of Bath's Prologue* (D 727–32) concerns Socrates and his shrewish wife Xanthippe (Xantippa):

> No thing forgot he the care and the woe
> That Socrates had with his wives two
> How Xantippa cast piss upon his head
> This silly man sat still as he were dead
> He wiped his head, no more durst he sayn,
> But 'Ere that thunder stint, cometh a rain!'

Shakespeare likewise used the word without reservation:

> ... I do smell all-horse-piss; at which my nose is in great indignation
>
> *The Tempest* (IV. i. 199–200)

> He had not been there ... a pissing while, but all the chamber smelt him
>
> *Two Gentlemen of Verona* (IV. iv. 19–21)

> I charge and command that, of the city's cost
> The pissing conduit run nothing but claret wine,
> The first year of our reign
>
> *The Second Part of Henry VI* (IV. vi. 2–5)

That the word had no suggestion of impropriety about it is spectacularly demonstrated by its use in the King James' Bible where it is used several times. In the First Book of Samuel for example the phrase 'any that pisseth against the wall' is an indirect way to refer specifically to men. (The New English Bible translates the expression less picturesquely as 'a single mother's son'.)

The word was even used in children's fairy tales. The following passage is taken from a 1621 version of Tom Thumb. The giant is making sure that Tom fully appreciates his great size: '... I can blow down a Steeple with my breath, I can drown a whole Town with my pisse ...'.

In *Gulliver's Travels* Swift relates how Gulliver quenched a fire in Lilliput by pissing on it.

The *Oxford English Dictionary* quotes some other usages:

> But as for Mony yt ys pyssyd on the walls. [i.e. money is squandered.] (1471)

> They are pestilent fellows, they speake nothing but bodkins, and pisse vinegar. (1602)

> There are some Quacks, as Honest Fellows as you would desire to Piss upon. (1700)

The flower that is now known as a dandelion used to be called a *piss-a-bed*, as indeed it still is in some dialects. The name refers to its diuretic properties. These properties are also known to the French: they call the flower a *pisse-en-lit*.

To their credit, most Europeans are consistently less mealy-mouthed than the British when it comes to bodily functions. A French urinal is unashamedly a *pissoir*, and the well-known Brussels statue of a little boy urinating is proudly known as the *Mannekin Pis*.

PISTOL

(*col.*) *The penis.*

This is one of the many English names for weapons which are also used for the male genitals (see WEAPON).

Shakespeare used it as the name of one of his best-known characters, and made the most of its double meaning. For example, in *The Second Part of Henry IV* (II. i. 54–5) a character observes that 'Pistol's cock is up', and later (II. iv. 112) Falstaff says 'Welcome, Ancient Pistol . . . do you discharge upon mine hostess'.

PIZZLE

(*col.*) *The penis.*

Used of animals' genitals since the early sixteenth century, the word is sometimes also applied to human ones. The original edition of the *Oxford English Dictionary* described the word as 'dialect or vulgar', but the latest supplement omits this description.

The word has a secondary meaning of 'whip' or 'flogging instrument', a natural consequence of the traditional use of bull's pizzles for flagellation.

In *The First Part of Henry IV* (II. iv. 248–52) Falstaff addresses Prince Hal, who has just described him as a huge hill of flesh:

'S blood, you starveling, you elf-skin, you dried neat's tongue, you bull's pizzle, you stock fish! O! For breath to utter what is like thee; you tailor's yard, you sheath, you bow case, you vile standing tuck.

Although these terms are used ostensibly to mean that Hal is thin and weedy, several of them also bear the secondary meaning of 'prick'.

PLACKET

(*col.*) *The female pubic area.*

This meaning stems from the word's conventional usage. In Standard English a placket is a slit at the top of a skirt or petticoat which makes it easier for the wearer to put it on and take it off. The word was once used also for petticoats and aprons, and also for women in general.

The proximity of plackets and female genitals was an easy source of ribald humour to Shakespeare. In the following examples the word is used with obvious sexual innuendo:

> . . . Cupid . . . prince of plackets, king of codpieces.
>
> *Love's Labour's Lost*, (III. i. 180)

> Keep thy foot out of brothels, thy hand out of plackets . . .
>
> *King Lear* (III. iv. 97–9)

> Is there no manners left among maids? Will they wear their plackets where they should bear their faces . . .
>
> *The Winter's Tale* (IV. iv. 253–5)

Though mini-skirts are generally thought to have been an invention of the 1960s, the following quotation cited in the *Oxford English Dictionary* and dated 1661 suggests otherwise:

> The extent of her placket is always lower than her smock, and that comes but an inch lower than her navel.

PLOUGH

(*col.*) *To copulate with a woman.*

This age-old metaphor, familiar to the Romans, belongs to a family of agricultural terms transferred to sexual activities. Others include *irrigate* and *dibble* (a dibble is a digging tool). See also SEED.

Shakespeare uses the metaphor in *Antony and Cleopatra* (II. ii. 240–42) where Agrippa says of Cleopatra 'Royal wench! She made great Caesar lay his sword to bed: He plough'd her, and she cropt'. In Bowdler's expurgated version, however, the references to ploughing and cropping were thought too strong and were omitted.

POKE

(*col.*) *See* WEAPON.

PONY AND TRAP

(*col.*) *Crap.*

Like many examples of Cockney rhyming slang this one is often reduced to one word, in this case *pony*.

POOF, also POOVE

(*col.*) *A male homosexual.*

Although generally thought to be Australian in origin, this word was first recorded in England in the middle of the nineteenth century. Numerous variations such as *pooftah*, *poofter*, *pofter*, and *pufter* do, however, appear to have originated in Australia. In Australian rhyming slang a *poof* may also become an '*orse's* '*oof*.

The earliest forms of the word seem to be derived from the word *puff* meaning to flatter extravagantly. We still use it in this sense when for example we talk about *advertising puffs*. It was apparently once much used in theatrical circles and it is from there that its new meaning seems to have developed.

POPPYCOCK

Nonsense.

Now in quite widespread use, this is a conveniently sanitized spelling of the word. It was apparently related to the Dutch *pappekak*, a more natural English rendering of which would be '*pappy-cack*', i.e. 'soft shit' (see CACK).

Pox

Venereal disease, especially syphillis.

To distinguish it from *smallpox* this complaint was known in the past as the *great pox*, or the *French pox*.

The term can also be used as an expression of disparagement or contempt. Shakespeare, in *Cymbeline* (II. i. 17–18), has Cloten remark 'I am not vexed more at any thing in the Earth. A pox on't . . .'. The sense is exactly the same as that of the more respectable *a plague on it!*

Pox is simply an alternative spelling of *pocks*. A pock in this sense is a small bag of puss, such pustules being a common characteristic of both the great pox and smallpox. Subsequent scars are known as *pock marks*.

Since ancient times the word *pock* has been applied to various types of bag. For example, the small bags sewn into clothing are *pocks*, but to emphasize that they are small they are called *pockets*.

Prat, also Pratt

(col.) An incompetent fool.

This usage presumably stems from the world's original meaning, which was 'buttock'. It has been well documented as slang since the sixteenth century.

An influence which may have assisted in the development of the new meaning may have been the Scottish word *prat*. Apparently quite distinct in origin, this has been used for a thousand years or so to mean 'trick' or 'prank'. The corresponding verb *prat*, to trick or fool, is similar in meaning to the modern expression to *prat about* or *prat around*, meaning to play the fool.

Prick

(col.) The penis.

The word is of ancient ancestry with its original meaning of sharp projection or point. It had already borne this meaning for over a thousand years before it was first recorded as a euphemistic name for the penis. Many terms for the penis make reference to it as an instrument for pricking or piercing. A few examples are *thorn*, *thistle*, and *needle*; see WEAPON for others.

In the Middle Ages the Standard English word for a penis was *PINTLE*. Since that time it has gradually fallen out of favour, being increasingly regarded as improper. By the seventeenth century *PRICK* and *COCK* had taken over as the new standard terms. Both of these words were themselves soon to fall into disfavour as *YARD*, and later *PENIS*, replaced them as the terms favoured by respectable society.

Ironically the word *pintle* is now so little known that it is unlikely to offend anyone. It is therefore curious to the modern eye to read a passage quoted in the *Oxford English Dictionary* and dated 1655: 'The Frenchmen call this Fish the Ass's Prick, and Dr Woton termeth it grossly the Pintle Fish'.

In another quotation we learn that the pineal gland, a part of the brain which resembles a pineapple or a penis-end depending on the disposition of one's imagination, was once known as the *Prick of the Brain*. The plant now generally known as a stone-crop was traditionally called a *prick-madam*, as indeed it still is in many dialects.

By 1785, however, sensitivities were acute and Grose was willing to have the word printed in his *Dictionary of the Vulgar Tongue* only as p—k.

By the early nineteenth century it was regarded as thoroughly offensive, and it is only since this time that the word has been used as an insult. It is interesting that words associated with sex have been used as popular insults only since prudes tried to stop them being used at all.

In earlier times the names for the genitals were sometimes affectionately applied to young people of the appropriate gender. Even now a boy or a man might, without offence, be called *cock*. In the following quotation, cited in the Oxford English Dictionary and dated 1671, *prick* is used in a similar way:

> One word alone hath troubled some, because the immodest maid soothing the young man, calls him her Prick . . . He who cannot away with this, instead of 'my Prick', let him write 'my Sweetheart'.

Clearly the prudes were already moving in, even at this early date.

Prudery has been responsible for the omission of many ancient proverbs from supposedly comprehensive reference works. One such is the sagacious observation that 'a standing prick has no conscience'.

117

PRIVY

See LAVATORY.

PROSTITUTE

As a noun, a whore; as a verb, to sell sexual services.

The word is based upon Latin elements which together mean 'to set before'. The underlying idea is that prostitutes are people who set themselves before potential customers.

Both noun and verb were introduced in the sixteenth century, but Shakespeare used only the verb. In *Pericles* (IV. vi. 189–91) Marina says to Boult:

> ... take me home again,
> And prostitute me to the basest groom
> That doth frequent your house.

Anglo-Saxon names for a prostitute included *cwene* and *hore*, which we still have as *QUEAN* and *WHORE*. Other terms accumulated throughout the Middle Ages, and by the sixteenth century there was a wide range of alternatives.

According to Dr Robert Burchfield, the Chief Editor of the Oxford dictionaries, the following synonyms for prostitute were current by the sixteenth century:[8] *baggage* (see BAG), *cat, cockatrice, cony* (see CUNNY), *courtesan, DOXY, drab, driggle-draggle, flirt-gill, hackney, HARLOT, hiren, hobby-horse, laced mutton, limber, loon, minx, mort, mutton, public woman, pucelle, PUNK, stale, stew, street-walker, strumpet, tomboy,* and *WAGTAIL.*

In the seventeenth century these were joined by: *buttock, cousin, CRACK, customer, fireship, flap, lady of pleasure, marmalade-madam, night walker, NYMPH, prostitute, pug, strum, tomrig, town-woman, vizard,* and *waistcoateer.*

The eighteenth century was quieter and saw the introduction of: *demi-rep, fille de joie, lady of easy virtue, rake,* and *woman of the town.*

First recorded in the nineteenth century were: *buer, chippy, cocotte,*

---

[8] Robert Burchfield, *Fair of Speech* (see Bibliography).

demi-mondaine, fallen woman, flagger, flapper, HOOKER, horizontal, horse-breaker, pick-up, scarlet woman, TART, and *unfortunate.*

Only since this century have we used the terms: *BRASS NAIL, broad, call girl, demi-vierge, demi-virgin, hostess, hump, LAY, make, model, MUFF, pavement princess, scrub, scrubber,* and *SLAG.*

PUDDINGS

Guts, intestines, entrails, bowels.

This meaning of the word, the original one, is now rarely intended. Indeed the threat of '*letting out someone's puddings*' would probably not now be understood, though it once promised disembowelment.

Generations of schoolchildren have ingenuously been taught that Pudding Lane, where the Great Fire of London started in 1666, was so called because sweets and desserts were prepared there. In fact *Pudding Lane* was so called because butchers from the nearby market in Eastcheap disposed of the unwanted entrails of slaughtered animals by carting them down this lane to tip into the Thames.

Sausage shaped foods were also known as *puddings.* This was a natural extension of the word's meaning, not only because of the similarity in shape, but also because intestine walls, when cleaned, have always provided the best sausage skins. *Black puddings* are 'puddings' in this sense of the word.

At a later date any mixed food cooked or served in such skins, whether savoury or sweet, came to be called *puddings*; and later still even the requirement for the involvement of skins was dropped, so providing the present meaning of the word.

Despite the changes that have taken place in the word's meaning over the centuries, we do still have the odd reminder that puddings have some atavistic connection with the belly. One might, for example, hear that a pregnant woman has a *bellyful of marrow pudding*, or that she is in the *pudding club*.

PUDENDUM

The genitals.

The term is generally applied to the female genitals, in which case the full form is *pudendum muliebre*.

Pudendum is borrowed from Latin, in which language it means 'that of which one should be ashamed'. Its use as an acceptable alternative to native English terms which are now taboo casts considerable light on attitudes to sex in Western culture.

The same Latin root appears in the word *impudent*. To be impudent is to be without shame. Shakespeare used *pudent* to mean 'appropriately modest'.

PUNK

(*col.*) *Prostitute, beggar, or drop-out.*

This is a very old word and has supported literally dozens of meanings over the centuries. The most familiar one nowadays is that associated with a youthful fashion of the mid 1970s. Another familiar meaning is the one found in dated American gangster films. Both are offshoots of the old meaning of 'beggar' or 'ne'er-do-well'.

Shakespeare was familiar with the word and its meaning of prostitute. In *Measure for Measure* (v. i. 179–80) he wrote: 'She may be a punk; for many of them are neither maid, widow, nor wife'.

PUSSY

(*col.*) *The female genitals.*

The word has been used in this sense since at least the seventeenth century.

In conventional use it is applied to cats, and so exactly parallels the French *chat/chatte* which shares the same pair of meanings.

Q

QUAINT

Cunt.

In some north-country dialects this sense may still be found, although it is now hardly ever encountered in mainstream English. In the past the word was also written *queinte*, *quaynte*, *quainte*, or *coynte*.

The earliest example quoted in the *Oxford English Dictionary* is dated around 1330: 'Hir queynt aboven hir knee, Naked the knightes knew'. The word was used a number of times by Chaucer. The following example is taken from *The Miller's Tale* (A 3276–9), where Nicholas takes a direct approach to seeking Alison's favours:

> And privilly he caught her by the queynte
> And said 'unless I have my will
> For dear love of thee, leman, I spill [die]
> And held her hard by the haunchbones . . .

The word is also used in *The Wife of Bath's Tale*, where the good wife refers to her favourite organ not only as a *queynte* (D 331–2), but also a *quoniam* (D 608), *bele chose* (beautiful thing) (D 447), and *chamber of Venus* (D 618).

By the seventeenth century the word was already being avoided and does not, for example, appear anywhere in Shakespeare's works. Andrew Marvel, however, seems to have been prepared to use it, though only ambiguously. The following passage is taken from a poem 'To His Coy Mistress' written in the middle of the seventeenth century:

> . . . But at my back I always hear
> Time's winged chariot hurrying near
> And yonder all before us lie
> Deserts of vast eternity

Thy beauty shall no more be found
Nor, in thy marble vault, shall sound
My echoing song; then worms shall try
That long preserved virginity,
And your quaint honour turn to dust
And into ashes all my lust
The grave's a fine and private place,
But none, I think, do there embrace.

In the late nineteenth century the word was still in circulation. Sir Richard Burton used it in his 1888 translation of *The Arabian Nights*, though he spelled it *coynte*.

Another meaning of *quaint* is 'known' (hence to *acquaint*, to 'become known'). This connection between knowledge and sex is implicit in many words. The word *KNOW* itself bears this double meaning, and *conceive* has a similar duality; it can mean either to form in the mind or to form in the womb. Again *CUNT* and *CUNNY* are related to *cunning*, the original meaning of which was 'knowing' or 'knowledgeable'. This duality also occurs in other Indo-European languages, and even in unrelated languages such as Hebrew.

QUEAN

(col.) A male homosexual.

The word is often mistakenly spelt 'queen', though *queen* is actually a quite different word.

The two terms have been distinguished since ancient times. The one now spelled *queen* was *cwen* in Anglo-Saxon times, and the other, now spelled *quean*, was *cwene*.

Cwene was a word applied to low women and prostitutes, which is exactly how its modern equivalent *quean* was used until this century, when it was taken over by male homosexuals.

The word *GAY* has been appropriated in much the same way within the last few decades.

QUIM

(col.) The female genitals.

Rescued by modern pornographic literature, this ancient word had fallen into obscurity earlier in this century.

It may be related to the Anglo–Saxon *cweman* and hence to *cwithe* meaning 'womb', or possibly to the Celtic *cwm*, a cleft or valley. Although the first explanation is by far the most likely, the second is supported by the large number of words for a cleft or gap which are used as euphemisms for the vagina (see CRACK).

R

RAG, TAG AND BOBTAIL

The rabble, the common herd.

The expression is a corruption of the older *rag-tag and bobtail* (or *tag-rag and bobtail*). A *rag-tag* was a low ragged servant, and a *bobtail* or *WAGTAIL* a common prostitute.

A number of relatively recent entertainments for children have names which are based on much older expressions or titles now almost forgotten (the original *Tom and Jerry*, for example, date from 1821). When *Rag*, *Tag*, and *Bobtail* were selected as names for characters in a 1950s children's television programme the earlier meanings had presumably already faded from the popular memory.

RASPBERRY

(col.) A fart, or imitation fart.

This is another example of Cockney rhyming slang not generally recognized as such. The full version is *raspberry tart*.

RECTUM

The final section at the end of the large intestine.

The full form is *intestinum rectum*, which in Latin means 'straight gut'. The stem *rect-*, meaning 'straight' occurs in many English words including *rectitude* (straightness), *rectify* (straighten), and *direct* (set straight).

RICHARD THE THIRD

(*col.*) *A turd.*

An example of ambiguous Cockney rhyming slang, this phrase is sometimes used to mean 'bird'.

RIDE

(*col.*) *To copulate with.*

As a euphemism for copulation this word has been in continuous use since the Middle Ages. The only difference is that, whereas the metaphor once referred solely to riding a horse, it now sometimes concerns bicycle riding. A promiscuous woman, for example, is sometimes called a '*village bike*'.

Riding St George is an old term for sexual intercourse with the woman sitting on top of the man. It was commonly believed in earlier centuries that a boy conceived in such circumstances was likely to grow up to become a bishop.

Riding is one of several metaphors for sexual intercourse which make reference to forms of physical exercise. Others, all of which date back at least to Elizabethan times, include *jump*, *leap*, *climb*, *vault*, and *MOUNT*.

RING

(*col.*) *The female genitals, also the anus.*

This is a very common, and very old, metaphor.

Grose, in the *Dictionary of the Vulgar Tongue*, mentions the meaning of female genitals. He also recounts the following story about Carvel's ring:

> . . . Ham Carvel, a jealous old doctor, being in bed with his wife, dreamed that the Devil gave him a ring, which, so long as he had it on his finger, would prevent his being made a cuckold: waking he found he had got his finger the Lord knows where . . .

This story, told in the eighteenth century, was already centuries old.

Ring snatching is an expression, more common in the USA than the UK, for sexual intercourse.

ROBY DOUGLAS

(*col.*) *The anus.*

Now apparently obsolete, this was once popular naval slang.

The original Mr Douglas is unknown to us but Grose, in the *1785 Dictionary of the Vulgar Tongue*, suggested that he had 'one eye and a stinking breath'.

ROCKS

(*col.*) *See* BALLS.

RODGER, also ROGER

(*col.*) *To copulate with.*

The secret diary of William Byrd of Westover contains what appears to be the earliest record of this usage. On 26 December 1711 he wrote of his wife 'I rogered her lustily', and again 1 January 1712 'I lay abed till 9 o'clock this morning . . . and rogered her by way of reconciliation'.[9]

The origin of the term is uncertain, but the fact that the name *Roger* has traditionally been a common one for rams and bulls used for stud may provide a clue. Neither is it likely to be a coincidence that, like many other men's names, it is also used as a term for the penis (see JOHN).

[9] Quoted by Eric Partridge in his *Dictionary of Rhyming Slang* (see Bibliography).

Rollock

(*col.*) *Testicle*.

Apparently introduced only within the last thirty years or so, this term was presumably used at first as a nonsensical euphemism for *bollock*.

The two words most similar to *rollock* in pronunciation and spelling seem to be unrelated. *Rowlock*, pronounced 'rollock', is the name of a device on a rowing-boat for restraining the oars; and *rollick* is a verb meaning to frolic, sport, or revel.

Root

(*col.*) *As a noun, the penis; as a verb, to copulate*.

An older form of the verb is *rootle*.

The word is not found with indisputable sexual connotations before the nineteenth century. There are however a number of ambiguous occurrences before that in which sexual innuendo is probably intended. The following exchange, from *The Merry Wives of Windsor* (IV. i. 42–7), are riddled with double entendres typical of Shakespeare:

EVANS. . . . What is the focative case William?
WILLIAM. O vocativo, O.
EVANS. Remember, William; focative is caret.
MISTRESS QUICKLY. And that's a good root.
EVANS. 'Oman, forebear.

Whenever Shakespeare uses 'O' it is a good bet that the passage will be full of bawdy double meanings. Here, in addition to *root* (penis) there is *caret* (*carrot* = penis) and *focative* (fuck). Although there is no way of proving that these double meanings are intended, the passage would make precious little sense otherwise.

Sexual meanings of *root* are well established in Australia, but not in the USA. There the verb is more likely to mean 'to support': to *root* for a team is to support it vocally.

RUT

(*col.*) *To be sexually excited, also to copulate.*

In Standard English the word is applied to male deer who become sexually active during the annual *rutting season*. At this time of year they roar, and it is ultimately, though rather indirectly, from the Latin word for roaring, *rugire*, that the word rut is derived.

In *The Merry Wives of Windsor* (v. v. 13–16) Shakespeare makes clear the allusion to deer when Falstaff says:

> . . . I am here a Windsor stag, and the fattest, I think, i' th' forest: send me a cool rut-time, Jove, or who can blame me to piss my tallow. Who comes here? my doe?

(To *piss one's tallow* was to sweat, lose weight, or become exhausted.)

In *Pericles* (IV. iv. 8–9) the word is used without reference to deer:

> I'll do anything now that is virtuous; but I am out of the road of rutting for ever.

See also TUP.

S

SAPPHISM
See LESBIAN.

SCATOLOGY
Obscene literature.

This meaning is a secondary one. The word was originally used as the name of a once important branch of medical science which dealt with diagnosis by inspection of faeces.

The stem *scat-* is of Greek origin and means 'shit'.

SCREW
(col.) To copulate with.

Perhaps surprisingly, the word has had this meaning since the eighteenth century at least. Although it suggests an insensitive approach to sex, the word may not have had such rough associations when it was first used.

As a noun it is also used as a slang term for a prison warder and this usage may well be connected. The term is a contraction of *screw driver*, an old slang phrase for a skeleton key. The connection with sex is provided by the age-old use of terms for keys, locks, and lock picking as sexual metaphors. (See the Biblical quotation at HOLE.)

SCUT

(*col.*) *The female pubic hair, or genitals.*

The Standard English meaning of the word is 'tail', specifically the upright tail of an animal such as a hare, rabbit, or deer. The transfer of meaning to 'genitals' exactly parallels that of the word *TAIL* itself. (See also PENIS for a masculine parallel.)

Shakespeare was familiar with the word's double meaning, as is clear from *The Merry Wives of Windsor* (v. v. 13–18). Immediately after Falstaff likens himself to a rutting stag (see the quotation at RUT) he refers to Mistress Ford as his 'doe with the black scut!'

In the *1811 Dictionary of the Vulgar Tongue* the word is defined concisely as 'The tail of a hare or rabbit; also that of a woman'.

SEED

Semen, thus offspring.

This agricultural metaphor is used throughout the King James' Bible. Cruden's *Complete Concordance*[10] of 1769 notes that:

> Seed in scripture is taken [1] properly, for that thin hot spirituous humour in man's body, which is fitted by nature for the generation of mankind . . . [2] Figuratively, for that which is begotten . . .

In Leviticus (15: 16–18) any ambiguity is removed by referring specifically to the 'seed of copulation':

> And if any man's seed of copulation go out from him, then he shall wash all his flesh in water, and be unclean until the even.
> And every garment, and every skin, whereon is the seed of copulation, shall be washed with water, and be unclean until the even.
> The woman also with whom man shall lie with seed of copulation, they shall both bathe themselves in water and be unclean until the even.

It is now known that spermatozoa are generated in the testes, but Culpepper's book on anatomy published in 1668 notes that some

---

[10] Alexander Cruden, *A Complete Concordance to the Old and New Testament* (1769).

people 'attributed to the kidneys the preparation of seed, because hot kidneys cause a propensity to fleshy lust'.[11]

The agricultural imagery implicit in the word is exactly paralleled in other languages, for example Latin (see SEMEN) and Greek (see SPERM). It is also emphasized by the fact that the female genitals were sometimes known in the past as *seed plots*.

SEMEN

Sperm, the fluid generated by male animals which carries the spermatozoa.

The word is Latin. It meant simply 'seed' and could be applied equally to both plants and animal seeds, just like the native English word SEED itself.

SHAG

(*col.*) *To copulate with.*

Although this sense of the word is recorded only from 1788, it had probably been well understood for many centuries before that. The original meaning which had been recorded much earlier was to swing, waggle, or shake. Indeed the word is probably related to *shake*.

Throughout the Middle Ages the word was indifferently spelled *shag* and *shog*. Shakespeare favoured *shog*, and it is his form that appears in one of his most memorable lines: 'Will you shog off?' (*Henry V* [II. i. 47]).

Although the meaning seems to be clear enough to modern ears, such phrases do not establish for certain that Shakespeare's *shog off* exactly parallels the modern *fuck off*.

[11] Nicholas Culpepper and Abdiah Cole, *Bartholinus' Anatomy* (1668).

SHAGGER'S BACK

(*col.*) *Back ache.*

Australian in origin, this term may be applied to a wide range of back complaints. It is used irrespective of whether the condition was really caused by over-indulgence in sexual intercourse.

SHIT, also SHITE

(*col.*) *As a noun, excrement; as a verb, to excrete.*

This word is very old. It has close relatives in most germanic languages; for example, the corresponding verbs in Dutch, German and Old Norse are *schijten*, *scheissen*, and *skita*, respectively. All are descended from a single ancestor which must have predated the development of separate teutonic languages in northern Europe.

The English form is of Anglo-Saxon origin and was first recorded around a thousand years ago with the specific meaning of diarrhoea. It was Standard English for centuries, and even now still hovers near the border of acceptability. Indeed, it is still the standard term for excrement in most dialects, and there can be few English speakers who are not familiar with it. Nevertheless, things have changed a lot since the thirteenth century when Sherborne Lane in the City of London was known as *shitteborwelane*, apparently because it was the site of a privy.

Old compounds which survive from past centuries include *shit house*, and *shite-poke*, this latter being a name used in the USA for a type of heron, and in Canada for a bittern. In Lincolnshire dialect the common redshank was known as a *shit-your-breeches*.

Other compounds which are now little used include *shit-a-bed*, *shit-breech*, and *shit-fire*. *Shit-a-bed* is an alternative name for the *piss-a-bed*, now better known as a dandelion. A *shit-breech* was one known to be liable to befoul himself, and a *shit-fire* was one liable to lose his temper easily.

The adjective *shitty* is relatively recent, the older equivalent being *shitten*. In the *General Prologue* to the *Canterbury Tales* Chaucer likens a foul priest and a member of his flock to 'A shitten shepherd and a clean sheep' (A 504). In 1738, Swift, in 'Polite Conversation', makes the observation 'Why Miss, you shine this Morning like a shitten Barn Door'.

A common proverb for centuries was 'shitten luck is good luck' which apparently promised good fortune to anyone who accidentally trod in a pile of shit.

As an exclamation, *shit!* is exactly parallel to the German *scheisse!* and the ubiquitous French *merde!*

SHMUCK

(*col.*) *A fool or dupe.*

In Yiddish the word's literal meaning is 'penis'. The term has, however, been adopted into American English as an insult. Its extension in meaning exactly parallels that of the native English *PRICK*.

In fact the Yiddish *shmuck* appears to be simply a variation of *shmock* meaning 'ornament'. Apparently the penis was once thought of as some sort of decorative item. Like most Yiddish words, this one is derived from Old German, so it is no coincidence that the modern German *schmuck* also means 'ornament'.

Though widely used in American English, in its original Yiddish *shmuck* is regarded as highly impolite. To reduce the offensiveness a contracted form, *shmo*, is now sometimes used instead.

Incidentally, the original Jewish language, Hebrew, reputedly possesses no obscene words. To be thoroughly offensive its speakers have to borrow expressions from other languages.

SIRREVERENCE!

An exclamation traditionally used when a turd is encountered in a public place.

Sadly, this expression seems to be obsolete, except in dialect. It has been used for centuries and features in many historical works. It is a corruption of the phrase *save your reverence!*, a politeness once used to excuse any unseemly incident. It has no exact modern counterpart. Our nearest approximation is probably 'bless you!': *excuse (me)!*, *pardon (me)*, and *sorry!* being generally used only when the speaker is at fault.

In *The Comedy of Errors* (III. ii. 91–3), Shakespeare uses the expression figuratively. Speaking of an unsavoury woman, Dromio describes her as 'such a one as a man may not speak of, without he say "sir-reverence"'.

Since it was used to excuse piles of excrement, a natural extension of the use of the expression was as a euphemism for excrement itself. In *Romeo and Juliet* (I. iv. 40–42) Shakespeare uses the term in this way. Speaking to Romeo, Mercutio says: 'If thou art Dun, we'll draw thee from the mire of this sir-reverence love, wherein thou sticks't up to the ears'.

Richard Head in *The English Rogue* (1665) refers to a man '. . . sirreverencing in a paper, and running to the window with it'. Those who happened to be below would have been expected to watch out for themselves: the environmental health authorities were not as diligent as they are now.

SLAG

(col.) A promiscuous woman.

This meaning of the word has acquired wide currency only in the last few decades, though brothel keepers are known to have been called *slaggers* in the early years of this century.

In the nineteenth century the term had been applied to any objectionable or contemptible person, whether man or woman. Indeed, it is still used in this way in many parts of England.

Earlier, in the eighteenth and early nineteenth century, it had been applied to cowards and other generally unspirited people. Thus in the *1811 Dictionary of the Vulgar Tongue* a *slag* is defined as 'a slack mettled fellow, one not ready to resent an affront'. This nearly gives away the ultimate origin of the word, for it is almost certainly a variation of *slack*, as in *slack spirits* or *slack morals*.

SLIT

(col.) The female genitals.

This is one of a large family of words referring to the cleft of the external female genitals (see CRACK). The metaphor is very old.

The following extract is from the poem *Hesperides*, by Robert Herrick (1648):

> Scribble for whoredom whips his wife, and cryes
> He'll slit her nose, but blubb'ring she replyes:
> Good Sir, make no more cuts i'th' outward skin,
> One slit's enough to let Adultry in.

SLUT

A dirty or promiscuous woman.

In meaning this word has remained unchanged since the Middle Ages.

It is closely related to *slattern*, a word with an identical meaning, the ultimate root of which meant to spill, splash, or waste.

Like other European languages, English has a number of names for prostitutes which also suggest dirty habits and ragged dressing.

SNATCH

(col.) As a noun, the female genitals; as a verb, copulation.

This usage is many centuries old.

The *Oxford English Dictionary* quotes a number of examples dating back to the sixteenth century in which it is clear that a sexual meaning is intended, though it coyly regards them as allusions to the eating of snacks. The following example is dated 1592: '... what baudry is it he will not suffer, so he may have money and good cheer, and, if he like the wench well, a snatch himself'.

By the beginning of this century the word was almost obsolete, being restricted almost entirely to Yorkshire dialect. Since the 1950s, however, it has regained much wider usage.

SNOT

(*col.*) *Nasal mucus.*

A word of ancient ancestry, this was Standard English up until the last century. It now occupies that strange borderland between the acceptable and the unacceptable.

It belongs to a large family of English words associated with the nose which begin with the letters 'sn'. A few examples are *snout*, *snitch*, *snore*, *snuffle*, *snarl*, *sneeze*, *sniff*, *snivel*, *snort*, and *snuff*.

These words all employ the same onomatopoeic element. It was presumably recognized by our primitive ancestors, possibly even before the development of true human speech.

SOD

(*col.*) *A male homosexual.*

This is a contraction of the word *sodomite*, a sodomite being originally a resident of the city of Sodom near the Dead Sea.

The inhabitants of Sodom were believed to have practised unnatural sexual activities, and to have incurred the wrath of God as a result. The story is told in the Bible (Genesis, chapters 18 and 19).

SON OF A BITCH

(*col.*) *A contemptible person.*

This favourite American insult is of considerable antiquity. In an embellished form it even appears in the works of Shakespeare. In *King Lear* (II. ii. 22) Kent calls Oswald 'the son and heir of a mongrel bitch'.

See also BITCH and, for similar terms of abuse, WHORESON.

Sow

(col.) A woman.

This is one of many uncomplimentary names for women borrowed from the animal world (see BITCH).

The Latin word for a young sow, *porcella*, was also used to mean 'vulva'. The sea shell now generally known as a cowrie or venus shell was called a *porcellana* because of the resemblance of its opening to a vulva. (*Porcelain* is so called because its surface looks similar to that of the shell.)

Sperm

Semen.

This word, like *SEMEN* and *SEED*, is an agricultural metaphor. It was originally associated with the sowing of plant seed, and later, by analogy, to the 'sowing' of metaphorical seeds (*wild oats* for example).

The original Greek word *sperma* comes from the stem of the verb *speirein*, meaning to sow.

Spunk

(col.) Seminal fluid, sperm.

Originally this word meant a 'spark'. Over the centuries it developed a secondary meaning of 'spirit', an initial spark being thought of as providing the spirit of a fire. A spirited person, one with drive and courage, could therefore be said to have *spunk*. Oliver Goldsmith used the word in this sense in *She Stoops to Conquer* (1773): 'The squire has got spunk in him.'

In English, a connection is often made between, on the one hand, maleness and, on the other, drive, ability and power. This is reflected in words like *virile* ('manly' and 'lively'), *impotent* ('unable to sustain a penile erection' and 'powerless'), *emasculate* (to 'castrate' and to 'render powerless') and *KNACKER* (to 'castrate' and to 'exhaust'). So too, figuratively, to *have balls* is to have an unusual degree of courage. In Anglo-Saxon times the word *geweald* was used to mean both 'male genitals' and 'power'.

It is not surprising, therefore, that a word like *spunk* should be extended to provide a name for semen, the essential manly spirit, although this seems to have happened only within the last two hundred years or so.

The word *METTLE* has developed exactly the same double meaning of 'ability' or 'courage', on the one hand, and 'semen', on the other.

STALLION

(col.) A virile man, or one with a large penis.

Stallions have inordinately large penises, a well-known fact, which provides this obvious and ancient analogy.

According to the *Oxford English Dictionary* the earliest recorded use of the word as applied to a man occurred in 1305. The gist of the quotation is that a monk who wants to be a good 'stallion' can have twelve women a year.

Jack-asses also have a reputation for possessing large genitals. The Bible (Ezekiel 23: 19–20) records the sexual exploits of a lady called Aholibah; as the King James' version relates:

> . . . she multiplied her whoredoms, in calling to remembrance the days of her youth, wherein she played the harlot in the land of Egypt. For she doted upon her paramours, whose flesh is as the flesh of asses, and whose issue is like the issue of horses.

Here the word *flesh* is a euphemism for 'penis', and *issue* one for the ejaculation of semen.

The *1796 Dictionary of the Vulgar Tongue* records another meaning for the word *stallion*. According to it, a *stallion* was 'a man kept by an old lady for secret purposes'.

For other animal names applied to men see BULL.

STARK NAKED

Totally naked.

Stark in this phrase is a corruption of the word *start* meaning 'tail' and thus 'genitals' (see TAIL). *Stark naked* therefore literally means naked to the genitals. The more recent expression *stark bollock naked* emphasizes the importance of the genital region even further.

The spelling was changed to *stark* possibly because the word *start* was a little too explicit in increasingly prudish times, or more likely because the word was already obsolescent and the phrase *start naked* no longer seemed to make sense. (The word *start* meaning 'begin' is unrelated.)

Although *start* has fallen out of use in popular speech, it still appears in certain old names. The bird known as a *redstart* for example is so called because of its red tail, and around the coast of Britain are a number of tail-like promontories with names like *Start Point*.

STICK

(col.) Penis.

This term refers to the fancied similarity in shape between an erect penis and a stick. The same analogy is implicit in other names for the penis such as *rod*, *pole*, *wand*, *staff*, *shaft*, *poker*, *spar*, and *YARD*.

Since the eighteenth century the basic *stick* metaphor has been embellished to provide expressions such as *cream stick* and *sugar stick* (the female genitals being known as a *sugar bowl*).

In the nineteenth century these terms were supplemented by *copper stick*, an expression which doubled as a name for a policeman's truncheon. A more recent form, *giggle stick*, is sometimes claimed to be Cockney rhyming slang for 'prick', although this explanation is rather doubtful. Yet another variation, *rhythm stick*, was brought into common use by Ian Dury's popular song 'Hit Me With Your Rhythm Stick'.

The expression *liquorice stick*, used for a black penis, was coined in the last couple of decades, apparently by homosexuals in the USA.

Gear stick and *joy stick* are another two recent metaphors for 'penis'.

STONES

Testicles.

For centuries this was the Standard English term.

It was used consistently throughout the King James' Bible of 1611. In Deuteronomy (23: 1), for example, it is stated that 'He that is wounded in the stones, or hath his privy member cut off, shall not enter into the congregation of the Lord.' Again in Leviticus (21: 16–24) we learn that those who should not 'approach to offer the bread of his God' include dwarves, the crooked backed, the blind, the lame, those with flat noses, those with 'any thing superfluous', and men who have their stones broken.

Job (40: 15–17) contains a description of an unusual character called Behemoth and his prodigious genitals:

> Behold now Behemoth, which I made with thee; he eateth grass as an ox.
> Lo now, his strength is in his loins, and his force is in the navel of his belly.
> He moveth his tail like a cedar: the sinews of his stones are wrapped together.

The exact meaning and relevance of this passage has puzzled commentators for centuries, though it is known that when it was written the word sinew meant 'mainstay' or 'chief supporting force'. It is also clear that *navel* is a euphemism for 'genitals' (see NAFF), and that *tail* means penis (see TAIL). In any case we do not come across many Behemoths nowadays.

Punning on this old meaning of *stone* is the expression *stone fruit*, meaning 'children', and the description *two stone underweight*, applied to eunuchs. In *Cymbeline* (II. iii. 33) Shakespeare refers to 'The voice of an unpaved eunuch'. Here the word unpaved is a pun: to be unpaved is to be without paving stones; in other words the eunuch is a man without stones.

Having abandoned *stones* as the Standard English in favour of *testicles*, we have now taken to calling them *rocks*.

STREWTH!

(*col.*) *An exclamation.*

This is a common, though etymologically incorrect, variation of *STRUTH!*

STRUTH!

(*col.*) *An exclamation.*

Still in common use, especially in Australia, this is a very old disguised oath (see OATH). It is a corruption of the expression *God's truth!*

STUFF

(*col.*) *To copulate with a woman.*

Although this term has a modern ring, as usual Shakespeare anticipated it. The following exchange occurs in *Much Ado About Nothing* (III. iv. 56–60):

> HERO. These gloves the Count sent me; they are an excellent perfume.
> BEATRICE. I am stuft, cousin; I cannot smell.
> HERO. A maid, and stuft! There's goodly catching of cold.

SUCKHOLE

(*col.*) *Toady, sychophant.*

Chiefly Australian, this lucid expression is comparable to traditional terms such as *arse-licker*, *bum-crawler*, and *brown-nose*. (See also KISS MY ARSE.)

Undue deference for some reason seems to attract names with unsavoury bodily associations. In addition to those already mentioned common examples are *catch-fart*, *cock-sucker*, *lickspittle*, and *toady* (a toady was originally a toad-eater). *Sychophant* may well properly belong to this list as well. (See FIG.)

SWEAR-WORD

A taboo word, one generally regarded as improper.

The practice of swearing originally involved the taking of an oath. In swearing an oath it was customary to use the name of a supernatural being (see GOD). Such names were supposed to be used only with reverence, and only in appropriate circumstances. In the Middle Ages, however, it became common practice to use them as exclamations. We do much the same even today with exclamations such as *good God!*, *Christ almighty!*, and *Jesus wept!* Alternatively we might call upon St Peter (*for Pete's sake!*) or St Michael (*for the love of Mike!*).

To avoid using swear-words in improper circumstances it was common practice to disguise them (see OATH for examples). As sensitivities increased it became necessary, especially in the traditionally puritanical United States, to disguise other words. Thus *Hell* became *Heck*; *damn*, *darn* or *dash*; *damnation*, *tarnation*; *Lord*, *lawks*; and *bloody*, any of *bally*, *ruddy*, *bleeding*, *blooming*, *blinking*, or *blessèd*. A *bastard* became a *basket*, a *bugger*, a *beggar*, and *bollocks*, *rollocks*.

By the last century the language had become liberally sprinkled with such totally meaningless terms. It was fairly natural to extend the meaning of the expression *swear-word* to any prohibited or otherwise unacceptable term. As words associated with sex and excretion became increasingly taboo they took over as the most common sort of 'swear-word'.

SWIVE

To copulate with.

Spelled *swyve* by Chaucer, this was the Standard English term for copulation. At the end of *The Miller's Tale* (A 3850–4) Chaucer sums up as follows:

> Thus swyved was this carpenter's wife,
> For all his keeping and his jealousy;
> And Absolon hath kissed her nether eye;
> And Nicholas is scalded in the towte [anus].
> This tale is done, and God save all the rowte [company].

Again, in *The Reeve's Tale* (A 4265–6) Aleyn boasts:

... I have thrice in this short night, swyved the miller's doughter
bolt upright ...

Since the Middle Ages the word has gradually fallen out of use in
mainstream English, though even now it still enjoys limited currency
amongst scholars and students of Middle English.

It is ultimately related to the German *schweben*, to hover.

SYPHILIS

A venereal disease.

The word was coined in 1530 by Girolamo Fracastoro, a physician
in Verona. He used it in a poem entitled *Syphilis sive Morbus Gallicus*
(Syphilis or the French Disease).

The hero of the poem was a shepherd called *Syphilus*, supposedly
the first person to suffer from the disease. His name is often said to
be derived from two words meaning 'together' and 'love', but it is
more likely to have been based on words meaning 'pig-lover'. There
is further doubt as to whether in this context the word 'pig' is to be
taken literally or as a euphemism for female genitals. Italian women
referred to their genitals as 'piggies' (see SOW).

T

TAIL

(col.) The genitals.

The original meaning of this word seems to have been 'hair', specifically a tuft of hair, and hence an animal's *tail*. However, it soon acquired a secondary meaning of 'rump', and thence the genital regions, both male and female. The American usage of the word, as in a *piece of tail* may sound modern, but its sexual connotations stretch back into prehistory.

Until the eighteenth century, *tail* was Standard English for the posterior or genitals; both meanings are retained in a number of English dialects. As applied to the female genitals it was probably influenced by the French word *taille* meaning 'notch'. The association is the same as that implied in many modern terms such as *cleft* and *cranny* (see CRACK).

Chaucer knew the meaning of 'genitals'. The following piece of sagacity is from the *Wife of Bath's Prologue* (A 466), where the meaning is clear enough when we remember that *lickorish* is essentially the same word as *lecherous*: 'A lickorish mouth must have a lickorish tail'.

The pun on *taille* also occurred to him. In *The Shipman's Tale* the merchant's wife says to her husband: 'I am your wife; score it upon my taille' (B2 416).

Tail and its homonym *tale* provided Shakespeare with a rich source of ribald ambiguity. The following, from *Othello* (III. i. 6–11), is a typical exchange:

CLOWN. Are these, I pray you, wind instruments?
FIRST MUSICIAN. Ay, marry, are they, sir.
CLOWN. O! Thereby hangs a tail.
FIRST MUSICIAN. Whereby hangs a tale, sir?
CLOWN. Marry, sir, by many a wind-instrument that I know . . .

Again, from *The Two Gentlemen of Verona* (II. iii. 49–53):

PANTHINO. Why dost thou stop my mouth?
LAUNCE. For fear thou shouldst lose thy tongue.
PANTHINO. Where should I lose my tongue?
LAUNCE. In thy tale.
PANTHINO. In thy tail!

Even more explicit is a line of Petruchio's from *The Taming of the Shrew* (II. i. 216) where he is exchanging bawdy puns with Kate: 'What! With my tongue in your tail? Nay, come again: Good Kate, I am a Gentleman'.

Old compounds incorporating the word *tail* include *WAGTAIL* and *bobtail*, both meaning 'lewd woman' or 'prostitute'; *draggle tail*, meaning 'dirty prostitute'; and *plug tail* and *tickle tail*, both meaning 'penis'. See also BRASS NAIL.

TAMPON

A plug of cotton inserted into the vagina to control menstrual bleeding.

This is just one specialized meaning of the word. In general it can be applied to any pack of material used to plug a bleeding wound or orifice.

It is related to the verb *tamp* meaning to stop up a hole, or to ram home the charge in a barrel-loading gun.

TARSE

The penis.

This ancient word, written *teors* in Anglo-Saxon times, fell out of use centuries ago except in dialect.

It was used in early versions of the Bible, but fell victim to euphemism in later ones. For example, in The First Book of Samuel (18: 25), where Wyclif's 1382 version used it, the 1611 King James' version refers merely to *foreskins*:

... The King desireth not any dowery, but an hundred foreskins of the Philistines, to be avenged of the King's enemies ...

Other Anglo-Saxon words for the male genitals have also fallen into disuse. Amongst them are *gesceapu*, 'a shape'; *getawa*, 'equipment' (cf. TOOL); and *geweald*, 'power' (see SPUNK). On the other hand, some ancient terms are still in use. With slight changes in spelling they are as familiar now as they were a thousand years ago. Amongst them are *WEAPON*, *TAIL*, and even the euphemistic *limb*.

TART

(col.) A promiscuous woman.

Originally a term of endearment, this word has been attracting less and less attractive overtones ever since it was first used in the nineteenth century. In many rural areas, however, the older, less offensive, meaning still survives. Curiously, in Australia it is not perjorative except in compounds. Thus the expression *little tart* is likely to cause offence where the unadorned *tart* would not.

The earliest usage may have been rhyming slang, the full form being *jam tart*, rhyming with *sweetheart*.

It is interesting that in Victorian times women were often likened to sweet food. The terms *biscuit*, *cake*, and *confectionery* were, for example, all euphemisms for women. Also comparable is the older *buttered bun* (a woman who has sexual intercourse with one man immediately after another), and the more recent *crumpet* and *crackling*.

Metaphors likening sexual desires and activities to eating are remarkably common. Other typical examples include *sexual appetite*, having a *nibble*, and *eating* (*fur pie*), which means 'practising cunnilingus'.

TESTICLES, also TESTES

The male gonads, BALLS.

Testicle is a diminutive form of *testis*, the Latin word for a witness. The same basic form may be seen in many English words; for example, a witness's statement is *testimony*, and to make such a statement is to *testify*.

It has been suggested that testicles are so called because they 'bear witness' to a man's virility, but this explanation lacks the ring of truth.

A more probable explanation is that testicles were regarded as sacred objects upon which oaths were sworn. Being associated with the creation of life they were seen as sacred and magically potent. (See FASCINATE and, for the female equivalent, FIG.) They therefore provided a vehicle through which God could be called upon to bear witness to the oath.

It is known that in ancient times the accepted practice in certain cultures was to clutch male genitals when swearing a formal oath. A rather coy description of this is given in Genesis (24: 2–9):

And Abraham said unto his eldest servant of his house, that ruled over all that he had. Put, I pray thee, thy hand under my thigh; And I will make thee swear by the Lord, the God of heaven, and the God of earth, that thou shalt not take a wife unto my son of the daughters of the Canaanites, among whom I dwell . . . And the servant put his hand under the thigh of Abraham his master, and sware to him concerning that matter.

This procedure is reported only once in the rest of the Bible (Genesis 47: 29), again where a particularly solemn oath is being taken.

The practice, or close variations of it, continue to this day in various parts of the world. In India, for example, a similar procedure is carried out, and in countries like Italy, renowned for their attachment to primitive superstition, one may routinely see men in the street grabbing themselves by the testicles and uttering oaths. This behaviour might be triggered by the occurrence of even unremarkable incidents, such as the sighting of a nun. It almost certainly represents a vestige of an ancient and sacred tradition of oath taking.

TIT

(col.) A breast.

This is simply a variation of the word *teat*, a word which dates back for well over a thousand years. However, it is only in the last fifty years or so that it has adopted this spelling.

Since adopting this form the word has become confused with another one, also written *tit*, which was applied to any small object. Thus a *titmouse* is a small bird, a *tit-bit* is a trifle, and a *tom tit* a small person. Small horses and girls were known as *tits*; so in 1837 Lady Tavistock could note with approval that she thought the Queen 'a resolute little tit'.

The form *Titty* was also used as a name for girls and was applied especially to a sister. One of the girls in Arthur Ransom's *Swallows and Amazons* was called *Titty*. Because of confusion with *titty* meaning 'teat' the name is not now often heard in the UK, though it still flourishes in many European countries.

TOILET
See LAVATORY.

TOM TIT
(*col.*) *Shit.*

In the eighteenth and nineteenth centuries the term was used as a name for a small or otherwise insignificant person. Its present sense is due to its use as Cockney rhyming slang.

TOOL
(*col.*)*The penis.*

The metaphor is not new: in fact it can be traced back to Old Norse and may well date back to prehistoric times.

Shakespeare knew this sense and used it in *Henry VIII* (v. iv. 32–4): 'Or have we some strange Indian with the great tool come to court, the women so besiege us? Bless me, what a fry of fornication is at the door!'

In English it is common to liken the male genitals to various items of working equipment. For example, as well as a *tool*, a penis might be called an *instrument*, *chopper*, or *organ*. Sometimes the male genitals are collectively likened to a whole set of working equipment.

As well as *equipment* a man's genitals might be referred to as *apparatus*, *kit*, *gear*, and *tackle* (as in '*wedding tackle*' and '*block and tackle*'). In line with this sort of usage the *1811 Dictionary of the Vulgar Tongue* defines *tools* as 'The private parts of a man'.

The expression *to grind one's tool*, applied to a man means to copulate, and *tool grinder* is one of the many names for the female genitals.

Toss

(*col.*) *As a noun, the act of masturbation; as a verb, to masturbate.*

This sense seems to have developed from an older and more general meaning of the word: to 'accomplish easily'. To *toss off* a piece of work is to do it quickly and easily; and *not to care a toss* is to care so little that one is not prepared to make even the smallest effort.

The word has been used with its secondary meaning of 'masturbate' for centuries. The rake in *The Rake's Progress* (1735) for example '. . . Then drops into St Dunstan's Church, And take[s] a Toss-off in the Porch'.

Over the centuries various meanings of *toss* have become mixed up. For example, the expression *toss-pot* is now often regarded as somehow improper. In fact a *toss-pot* is a person who tosses off a drink, in other words one who downs it easily in a single draught.

Tummy Banana

(*col.*) *The penis.*

Recently popularized by Barry Humphries, this is one of a long line of humorous terms for the penis. Other examples, some of them mentioned elsewhere, are *one-eyed trouser snake*, *pork sword*, *beef bayonet*, *pink oboe*, *silent flute*, *sugar stick*, *love-muscle*, *sausage*, *plonker*, *tassel*, *bone*, *wanger*, and *winkle*.

TUP

(col.) To copulate with a female.

This is Standard English when applied to sheep, but has long been informally extended to human beings. Using an explicit metaphor in *Othello* (I. i. 88–9) Shakespeare has Iago say to Brabantio, referring to Othello: 'Even now, now, very now, an old black ram is tupping your white ewe'.

It is one of several terms for sexual intercourse borrowed from the animal world. Others include *RUT* (deer), *COVER* (horses), and *serve* (cattle and other large animals). Significantly, the corresponding male animal names (*ram*, *stag*, *stallion*, and *bull*) are all applied to sexually active men.

Other such words used of human beings include *mate*, a general purpose copulatory term, and *clicket*, the technical term for copulation between foxes.

In all probability the surname *Tupper* was originally conferred on men well known for their sexual appetites.

TURD

A piece of excrement.

This is a venerable word with close relatives in most Germanic languages. It has been Standard English since Anglo-Saxon times, but since the eighteenth century has been avoided in polite society. Even by the seventeenth century the synonym *dung* was generally preferred in formal writing.

The most likely theory as to its ultimate origin is that it is derived from an ancient Proto-Indo-European word meaning to twist or curl. The connection being well illustrated by the characteristic curl of a typical dog turd.

In Wyclif's 1388 version of the Bible, in the Second Book of Kings (18: 27), may be found the memorable line '. . . they eat their turds, and drink their piss with you', but by 1611, in the King James' version this had become '. . . they may eat their own dung, and drink their own piss with you'.

In the 1388 version, Isaiah (5: 25) reads '. . . the dead bodies of them were made as a turd in the midst of the streets . . .' (the earlier

(1382) version had referred to *dirt*, at that time an equally explicit term, see the entry at DIRT). By 1611, however, it was felt necessary to carry out some creative editing: '. . . their carcases were torn in the midst of the streets . . .'

Again in Wyclif's earlier version, Paul writes in his epistle to the Philippians (3: 8) that: '. . . All things . . . I deem as turds, that I win Christ'. In the King James' version this has become '. . . I . . . do count them [all things] but dung that I may win Christ'.

However, in the 1621 *History of Tom Thumb*, the earliest recorded version of the Tom Thumb fairy story in English, the word is clearly thought suitable for children's ears. Here Tom has been swallowed by a cow, and finds the environment less than convivial: 'But to conclude, the poor beast could not be delivered of her troublesom burden, till a laxative drink cast into her belly, had turned him out in a cowturd . . .'

By the late eighteenth century Grose in his *Dictionary of the Vulgar Tongue* clearly thought the word thoroughly improper and felt it necessary to write it as *t—d*, just as he used *sh—e* for *shite*. Under the entry at *T—d* may be found: '. . . He will never sh—e a seaman's t—d; i.e. he will never make a good seaman'.

Turd Burglar

(*col.*) *A male homosexual.*

This is a relatively recent expression which is generally used humorously. The implicit suggestion, that the purpose of the active partner is to secretly extract excrement from his passive partner, is a common theme in humorous slang. Less explicit examples are *chocolate bandit* and *chutney ferret*.

Twat, also Twot

(*col.*) *The female genitals.*

Though it is now a common word, it was marked as obsolete in the original edition of the *Oxford English Dictionary* (1933).

It was first recorded in the seventeenth century, although it is probably much older. One of the earliest written examples occurs in 'Vanity Of Vanities' (1660):

> So they talk't of his having a Cardinal's Hat,
> They'd send him as soon an Old Nun's Twat.

This led to one of the most spectacular misunderstandings of English letters ever. In the prudish nineteenth century, Robert Browning picked up the word, presumably having seen the above passage. Rashly he assumed that it denoted part of a nun's headgear. He subsequently caused himself considerable embarrassment by using it in his famous poem 'Pippa Passes'.

U

UNMENTIONABLES

Knickers, or other underwear.

This ridiculously coy expression may still occasionally be heard, though it really belongs to the last century.

In the early nineteenth century, even before the term was applied to underwear, it was used for ordinary trousers. Strange though it may now seem, when they were first introduced in the late eighteenth century trousers were regarded as at best preposterous and at worst positively indecent. Until then the accepted wear for men had been breeches.

Between 1790 and the middle of the nineteenth century, by which time they had become established as acceptable, trousers were given a succession of silly and evasive names. As well as *unmentionables*, they were called *inexpressibles, indescribables, unspeakables, ineffables, unexplicables, unwhisperables, innomonables, unutterables*, and *unhintables*.

Many of our extreme euphemisms, including most of these, originated in the USA where the parochial middle classes traditionally set the trends.

Such euphemisms, however, became almost universal at one time. Even Dickens used them. In *The Pickwick Papers* (ch. 16), for example, he wrote: 'Mr Trotter ... gave four distinct slaps on the pocket of his mulberry indescribables ...'.

URINE

Piss.

Adapted from the Latin *urina*, which had the same meaning, this is the currently acceptable term in English. The corresponding verb is *urinate*, though this is already too common for the medical fraternity who prefer to *micturate*.

Ultimately the Latin word is derived from one that meant 'water'. To this extent the Latin exactly parallels the native English *water*, as in the expression *to make water* (see WATER, TO MAKE). The phrase *to make water* was the standard expression until the last few decades, and in 1976 Lord Denning felt it necessary to use both the English and Latin terms to ensure that a jury knew what he was talking about. He related that a certain Mr Hook 'went into a side street near the market and there made water, or "urinated" as it is now said'.[12]

In classical Latin the verb *urinare* meant 'to dive', which explains why the English word *urinator* originally meant 'diver'.

In *The Merry Wives of Windsor* (III. i. 13–15), Shakespeare used the word *urinals* to mean testicles. Threatening in his Welsh accent to knot Caius's testicles around his head, Sir Hugh Evans says: 'I will knog his urinals about his knave's costard when I have goot opportunities for the 'ork'.

[12] *R* v. *Barnsley LBC ex parte Hook* [1976] 3 All England Reports 452–455.

V

VAGINA

The internal female genitals.

As might be expected, this word is Latin. In Latin it originally meant 'sheath' or 'scabbard', so its present meaning in English puts it into that large category of terms which liken the genitals to items of weaponry (see WEAPON).

VENEREAL

Associated with sex.

Originally the word was associated with love rather than sex. The present meaning has arisen because of its usual association with disease; *venereal disease* is thought of as a sexually transmitted disease rather than a lovers' disease.

In Shakespeare's *Titus Andronicus* (II. iii. 37–9) Aaron says:

> . . . No madam, these are no venereal signs:
> Vengence is in my heart, death in my hand,
> Blood and revenge are hammering in my head . . .

He is not denying that he has the symptoms of an unpleasant disease: he is denying that he is concerned with love.

The word *venery*, meaning sexual indulgence, shares the same ultimate root. This is itself closely related to *Venus*, the name of the Roman goddess of love.

VIRGIN

One, especially a woman, who has not yet had sexual intercourse.

This word is derived from the Latin *virgo*, which had exactly the same meaning. Hence the name of the constellation *Virgo*, the virgin.

Although not generally regarded as improper, the term does occasionally cause embarrassment. Every year a new set of schoolchildren encounter it in the Christmas story and want to know what it means. Apparently not all of them are given adequate explanations. Surveys in which adolescent girls are asked 'Are you a virgin?' invariably elicit a significant proportion of replies 'Not yet'.

VULGAR

Obscene.

This is an extension of the Standard English meaning of 'ordinary' or 'common'. It is the standard meaning that we use when talking about *vulgar fractions*: vulgar fractions are merely 'ordinary' fractions, rather than, say, decimal fractions. So too *vulgar Latin* was the form of Latin used by the common people, and the *vulgate Bible* was the one written for the masses.

The word is ultimately derived from the Latin *vulgus*, meaning 'the common herd'.

It is an unfortunate reflection on the masses that words for them frequently acquire uncomplimentary connotations. For example, they are sometimes contemptuously known as *hoi polloi*, an Ancient Greek expression which means 'the masses'. The word *mob* is an eighteenth century contraction of the Latin *mobile vulgus*, literally the 'fickle crowd'. In our native English we speak of *the great unwashed*.

Before reaching its present meaning vulgar had declined gradually. The sequence of successive meanings on the way down were roughly as follows: 'everyday', 'common', 'shallow', 'uncultured', 'uncouth', 'coarse', 'rude', 'offensive', and 'obscene'.

The word *common* is well on the way down the same path. From its original meaning of 'everyday' or 'widespread' it has already reached the 'uncouth' stage – 'don't do that, it's so common', 'he's such a common little man'.

Even the word *popular* has made a start: *popular newspapers* are contrasted with quality newspapers, and it is well known that anything described as *popular entertainment* simply cannot be worth the time of day.

VULVA

The external female genitals.

This is another word borrowed from Latin, and therefore veiled in classical decency.

In Latin it has both the specific meaning of 'uterus' and a more general one of 'wrapper'.

W

WAGTAIL

(*col.*) *A promiscuous man or woman.*

Here the element *tail* means 'genitals' (see TAIL). So a *wagtail* is literally one given to exhibiting his or her genitalia.

Shakespeare used the word in *King Lear* (II. ii. 68) where Kent calls Oswald a *wagtail*. It is also implied in *Titus Andronicus* (v. ii. 87–8) where Titus observes that '. . . the empress never wags but in her company there is a Moor'.

By the eighteenth century the term was more generally applied to women, specifically to lewd women and prostitutes.

WALLY

(*col.*) *A fool.*

In the East End of London this word has been used for a hundred years or so as a name for a dill cucumber. Because of the phallic appearance of such vegetables the word was also applied to penises, and like many names for a penis it has come to be used as a term of abuse.

Some support for this derivation is provided by the word *DILL*, another name for a pickled cucumber. It is also used as a term for a penis, and hence as a term of abuse.

WANK, originally WHANK

As a noun, a bout of masturbation; as a verb, to masturbate.

Although it is now a well-known and widely used word, there is no record of its use before this century and no very convincing suggestion as to its origin.

A hand is sometimes referred to as a *wanker's spanner*.

WATER CLOSET
See LAVATORY.

WATER, TO MAKE

To urinate.

Although *piss* was the Standard English for many centuries, this euphemism has also been in continuous use alongside it.

Shakespeare used the expression in *The Two Gentlemen of Verona* (IV. iv. 39–42) where Launce asks: '... When didst thou see me heave up my leg and make water against a gentlewoman's farthingale? Didst thou ever see me do such a trick ...'.

W.C.
See LAVATORY.

WEAPON

(col.) The penis.

There is an ancient and widespread association between sex and violence: an association which is reflected in the many names for weaponry which are also applied to the genitals. In Latin the word *telum* could mean 'weapon', 'tool', or 'penis'. As in many other languages, words for weapons such as daggers and swords were also used as names for the penis.

In English as well as the term *weapon* itself, there are those which liken the penis to a battering or chopping instrument: *club*, *pollaxe*, *ram-rod*, *STICK*, and *chopper*; those which liken it to a stabbing instrument: *dagger*, *sword*, *dirk*, *bayonet*, *pike*, *stake*, and *lance*; and those which liken it to a firearm: *PISTOL*, *gun*, and *bazooka*.

This symbolism extends to terms for sexual intercourse. As well as the general battering terms given under BONK, there are a number which reflect the stabbing theme: *impale*, *prong*, *thrust*, *stab*, *foin*, *prick*, and *poke*. Yet others continue the firearms analogy, likening ejaculation to a firing explosion; examples are *shoot*, *bang*, *fire*, and *discharge*.

WET SEASON

(*col.*) *A woman's menstrual period.*

This is another characteristically vivid Australian metaphor.

WHAM BANG THANK YOU MA'AM

(*col.*) *A very brief sexual encounter.*

This term originated in the USA, and is best known in the UK through its use in David Bowie's well-known song 'Suffragette City'. It divides neatly into *wham-bang*, meaning copulation and *thank you ma'am*, the leave-taking afterwards.

Wham bang is one of the numerous terms for sexual intercourse which rely on violent imagery (see BONK).

WHIRLIGIGS

(*col.*) *Testicles.*

For centuries the term *whirligig* was Standard English as the name of a children's revolving toy, and the 'testicles' meaning is simply an extension of this.

Words for various playthings have been transferred to the testicles over the centuries. Examples are *MARBLES* and *baubles*.

Other old playful terms for the testicles include *tallywags*, *twiddle-diddles*, and *bag of tricks*.

WHORE

A prostitute.

This ancient word has close relatives in most languages throughout northern Europe.

A thousand years ago it meant not 'prostitute', but 'adulterer', and before that it had meant something like 'sweetheart'.

WICK

(*col.*) *The penis.*

This is an example of rhyming slang, the full form being *Hampton Wick*, and the missing rhyme *prick*.

Wick is unusual as rhyming slang in that it is the second part of the full expression; usually the first is used, deliberately obscuring the meaning for the uninitiated. In fact *hampton* has been the more popular form until the last few decades, and there is no very good explanation as to why *wick* has displaced it.

The term enjoys widespread use in expressions such as *dip one's wick*, meaning to have sexual intercourse; and *get on one's wick*, really to *get on one's prick*, which means to get on one's nerves or to annoy.

WILLY

(*col.*) *See* JOHN.

WIND

Flatulence.

The word is often found in the expression to *break wind*, meaning to fart. This usage has a venerable history dating back to AD 1000 at least. It is a fairly obvious extension of the word's conventional meaning.

Isaiah (26: 18), in the King James' Bible, imaginatively describes disappointed expectations: 'We have been with child, we have been in pain, we have, as it were, brought forth wind . . .'.

Shakespeare refers to the breaking of wind in *The Comedy of Errors* (III. i. 75–6): 'A man may break a word with you, sir; and words are but wind; Ay and break it in your face, so he break it not behind'.

The currently accepted term for wind, *flatulence*, is derived from the Latin *flatus*, a word which also meant 'a blowing' or 'breathing'. The same root may be seen in other English words such as *inflate* and *deflate*.

WHORESON

(col.) A term of abuse comparable to 'bastard'.

Literally meaning *whore's son*, the term has been used since at least the ninth century. For some reason it has fallen almost into disuse, despite its obvious suitability for the spirit of the modern age.

Shakespeare used it in his plays on numerous occasions. The following are just a few of many examples:

. . . thou whoreson ass . . .

The Two Gentlemen of Verona (II. v. 44)

You whoreson peasant!

The Two Gentlemen of Verona (IV. iv. 46)

. . . You whoreson loggerhead!

Love's Labour's Lost (IV. iii. 202)

You whoreson villain!

The Taming of the Shrew (IV. i. 148)

Whoreson caterpillars!

The First Part of Henry IV (II. ii. 85)

You whoreson round man

The First Part of Henry IV (II. iv. 143)

Whoreson mad fellow

Hamlet (V. i. 181)

You whoreson cur!

Troilus and Cressida (II. i. 42)

. . . A whoreson jackanapes . . .

Cymbeline (II. i. 3–4)

Women who gave birth on sailing ships in earlier times often did so by the midship guns, where a degree of privacy might be obtained. When the father's identity was uncertain the ship's log would record the newborn child as a *son of a gun*. So this phrase also means much the same as *SON OF A BITCH*, *whoreson*, and also *BASTARD*. In each case the essential insulting charge is that of illegitimacy and a suggestion of immorality about the mother's personal life.

WOMB

The uterus.

In earlier times the word had a more general meaning of 'belly', 'stomach', or 'bowels', so it could be applied equally to men and women. The modern meaning displaced the older one some three hundred years ago.

This probably explains why, despite its Anglo–Saxon origins, the word has never been regarded as improper. It is used interchangeably with its Latin equivalent *uterus*. This is rather unusual for a native English word with sexual associations, even indirect ones.

Y

YARD

(col.) The penis.

Now archaic, and used only with deliberate humour, this was Standard English until the last century.

Originally the word denoted a shoot or stick, and thence a rod or staff. The original meaning developed in a number of ways. For example, the spar used on sailing ships to support a square sail is called a *yard*; and since sticks were used as measuring rods the word also came to denote a standard distance (now three feet, but originally varying from one part of the country to another).

The use of the word in its present sense stems from a fancied resemblance between a staff or pole and an erect penis (cf. STICK).

Its ancient respectability when used in this sense is illustrated by its use in Wyclif's version of the Bible of 1382. For example, God's instruction to Abraham to have himself circumcised (Genesis 17: 11) reads: 'Ye shall circumcise the flesh of the furthermost part of your yard'.

In the following exchange, from *Love's Labour's Lost* (v. ii. 661–3), Shakespeare makes the most of the potential for puns:

ARMANDO. I do adore thy sweet Grace's slipper.
BOYET. [*Aside to Dumaine*] Loves her by the foot.
DUMAINE. [*Aside to Boyet*] He may not by the yard.

YONI

The female genitals.

In its original language, Sanskrit, this word denotes a symbolic representation of the female genitals under which the Hindu god Sakti is worshipped.

It has recently gained a measure of popularity, being preferred to the native *CUNT*, which is now regarded as vulgar, and the educated *VAGINA*, which is thought too clinical.

Z

ZOUNDS!
An archaic expression.

Familiar through comic books and historical works, this is a disguised oath (see OATH). It is now usually pronounced to rhyme with 'hounds' but originally it would have rhymed with 'wounds'.

In fact it is a corruption of the expression *God's wounds!*, a reference to Jesus' crucifixion wounds.

BIBLIOGRAPHY

In addition to the works of Chaucer and Shakespeare, various translations of the Bible, and etymological dictionaries by Skeat, Onions, Weekley, and Klein, along with the *Oxford English Dictionary* and Supplements, the following were consulted in the preparation of this book:

Baker, Sidney J., *The Australian Language*. SUN (1986).

Barthel, Manfred, *What the Bible Really Says*. Souvenir Press (1982).

Cohen, A. (ed.), *The Soncino Chumash*. Soncino Press (1974).

Downes, William, *Language and Society*. Fontana (1984).

Enright, P. J. (ed.), *Fair of Speech*. Oxford University Press (1985).

Fairfield, Sheila, *The Streets of London*. Macmillan (1983).

Field, John, *English Field Names*. David & Charles (1982).

Franklyn, Julian, *A Dictionary of Rhyming Slang*. RKP (1981).

Grose, Francis, *A Classical Dictionary of the Vulgar Tongue* (Reprint of 1811 edition). Bibliophile Books (1982).

Howard, Philip, *The State of the Language*. Hamish Hamilton (1984).

Marckwardt, Albert H., *American English*. Oxford University Press (1958).

Opie, Peter and Iona, *The Classic Fairy Tales*. Granada (1980).

Orton, Harold and Haliday, Wilfrid J., *Survey of English Dialects*. University of Leeds (1961–1967).

Partridge, Eric, *Shakespeare's Bawdy*. RKP (1956).

Partridge, Eric, *Dictionary of Historical Slang*. RKP (1973).

Partridge, Eric, *Origins*. RKP (1979).

Partridge, Eric, *Slang Today and Yesterday*. RKP (1979).

Reaney, P. H., *The Origin of English Place Names*. RKP (1980).

Reaney, P. H., *The Origin of English Surnames*. RKP (1980).

Robertson, Stuart and Cassidy, Frederic G., *The Development of Modern English*. Prentice Hall (1954).

Rosten, Leo, *The Joys of Yiddish*. Penguin (1983).

Shipley, Joseph T., *The Origins of English Words*. Johns Hopkins University Press (1985).

Tannahill, Reay, *Sex in History*. Abacus (1981).

Trudgill, Peter, *Sociolinguistics*. Penguin (1984).

Weekley, Earnest, *Surnames*. John Murray (1917).

Weekley, Earnest, *The Romance of Words*. John Murray (1917).